Edited by the
**Dicastery for Communication**

Pope Francis

Why are you afraid?
Have you no faith?

# Extraordinary Moment of Prayer in Time of Pandemic

## Presided over by Pope Francis

**Sagrato of St Peter's Basilica**

Friday, 27 March 2020 at 6:00 p.m.

That day when evening came,
he said to his disciples,
"Let us go over to the other side."

Leaving the crowd behind,
they took him along, just as he was, in the boat.
There were also other boats with him.

A furious squall came up,
and the waves broke over the boat,
so that it was nearly swamped.

Jesus was in the stern, sleeping on a cushion.

The disciples woke him and said to him,
"Teacher, don't you care if we drown?"

He got up, rebuked the wind and said to the waves,
"Quiet! Be still!"

Then the wind died down and it was completely calm.

He said to his disciples, "Why are you so afraid? Do you still have no faith?"

They were terrified
and asked each other,
"Who is this? Even the wind and the waves obey him!"

(*Mark* 4:35-41)

"For weeks now it has been evening. Thick darkness has gathered over our squares, our streets and our cities; it has taken over our lives, filling everything with a deafening silence and a distressing void, that stops everything as it passes by; we feel it in the air, we notice in people's gestures, their glances give them away."

# Hands on the Helm of History

## Preface

"There is nothing stronger in the world than the prayer of the just person. The person who prays has their hands on the helm of history." Saint John Chrysostom, Bishop and Doctor of the Church between the fourth and fifth centuries, is the one who wrote this. At that troubled and difficult time from many points of view, that great shepherd taught that the true motor of life in the world is the praying heart: the helm of history is the hands of those who know how to turn their gaze to the Lord with profound faith and great humility.

Can we define any moment in the flow of the world's history as easy? Perhaps not. It certainly was not so for the first months of 2020 when an unpredictable pandemic affected almost all of humanity. During that time, precisely in the late afternoon of March 27, the Holy Father Pope Francis, repeated through words and gestures the deeply-rooted convictions of this ancient Bishop and Doctor: "The person who prays has their hands on the helm of history."

It was for that purpose that he convened the Church and, in a certain sense the entire world, asking that we lift our eyes all together to the Lord of time and of history – to first of all consider the mysterious course of existence through the heights of His Word, finding there meaning and hidden grace; then, to implore His help and mercy at a time of great human, material and spiritual affliction; finally, to bless the course of all humankind, inspired by the logic of the civilization of love.

"The person who prays has their hands on the helm of history." We have all learned this anew, observing the Holy Father as he ascended the steps of Saint Peter's Square, drenched with rain. We saw in him the man in prayer ascending toward God to stand confidently before Him, as the guide of a vast number of people and a faithful intercessor. We also learned it anew listening to the word of Truth and Life from the Gospel, and in the silence with which that Word became Light in our manifold darkness. We learned it once again looking with emotion on the Miraculous Crucifix of Saint Marcello's Church and the icon of the Madonna *Salus Populi romani* (Protectress of the Roman People) – eloquent and evocative images of the salvation offered to us by the One who died and rose for us and of that maternal care that tenderly bends over every type of human pain. Finally, we learned it in the Eucharistic adoration and in the great *Urbi et Orbi* benediction, when the Savior of the world touched all of humanity with a loving caress capable of redeeming, consoling and offering hope.

That late afternoon, Saint Peter's Square was empty, deserted. Incredibly deserted. And as quiet as ever. And yet, right there, the entire world was gathered, called together by a man dressed in white who, once again, repeated words to everyone without exception that were strong and persuasive, and with the humble power of images: "The person who prays has their hands on the helm of history."

He then reaffirmed it once again as he took his leave of the place of that huge prayerful gathering – silently and alone – as if to say to himself and to everyone along with the Psalmist: "I lift my eyes to the hills – from where will my help come? My help comes from the Lord, who made heaven and earth" (*Ps* 121:1).

**Msgr. Guido Marini**
Master of Pontifical Liturgical Celebrations

Part I

# The *Statio Orbis*

# Introduction

## Part I

What happened on March 27 in Saint Peter's Square?

Something both simple and huge happened. An extraordinary moment of prayer united the world. The images were powerful, dramatic. Many asked themselves questions regarding what they witnessed. But the most important thing that happened was not visible to the naked eye.

In various ways many sought a response, but in the end did not find one. We will, in fact, never understand the power of that moment using traditional methods of analysis. That would be like trying to understand poetry using the metric system.

We live at a time in which we risk being blinded – a short-sighted, myopic time. We are not capable of seeing essentials: a world transfigured in pain, the discovery of our own fragility, the need to look beyond, and to turn to God.

There are never answers to poorly asked questions. So, the focus of the question needs to shift. Where does the need to pray arise? Wherein lies the extraordinary quality of March 27? In the liturgy? In the camera angles? Or in the truth that it represented?

For weeks, it seemed that an evening had fallen without the prospect of daylight. For weeks, the world looked to Rome, to the Pope, to find answers in his words that did not focus on the number of victims. For weeks, Pope Francis had opened the doors of his little chapel, Santa Marta, to the entire world so that everyone could pray with him during the Mass and listen to his explanation of the readings. For weeks, he too had asked himself how to accompany this desert-crossing using symbolic actions capable of bearing light on it: his solitary pilgrimage on the Via del Corso to visit the Miraculous Crucifix, praying before the icon of Salus Popoli Romani, the recitation of the Our Father on the part of all Christians on the day on which many Churches recall the Annunciation to the Virgin Mary and the Incarnation of the Word. This was how the idea of an extraordinary moment of prayer took shape.

The first to speak publicly about it was Father Marco Pozza, prison chaplain of Due Palazzi prison in Padua, during a television show produced by the Italian Episcopal Conference on Rai1, an Italian television channel with the highest viewership.

He said, "I am the last priest on the planet. I live in a prison with people who have failed in life. I ask Pope Francis to perform a powerful gesture. ... A *Statio Orbis*,[1] which certain times has been done. I ask that he choose the day, the hour, the form. Perhaps he can be alone in Saint Peter's Square, or inside the Basilica ... and ask God through a prayer of liberation, a Mass, something. ... I ask Pope Francis to perform a universal action. Ask the Church to stop, ask the entire world to stand next to you. ... You possess the power of the word, you possess the power of symbol. Make us understand that Christ is there in this moment and that He is telling us something. You are a bridge for us. ... Do not leave us alone."[2]

That same day, Father Marco had written on his blog: "Last night, I dreamed about you, Pope Francis: you were really clear. And next to you, Mary's lamp was shining. I saw you silently slip out of Santa Marta. You were repeating '*Ave Maria, gratia plena, Dominus tecum*' in your inimitable Argentinian accent. She was just ahead of you and pushed the doors open for you – they were all locked. You went all the way into Saint Peter's Square under the obelisk which seemed to me like a finger pointing Heavenward. The square was empty, deserted, in an unusual state of besiegement. And you were there in the middle kneeling on the ground. You were there for a long time, in silence, hands folded, with those mystical features that I see in you when you pray. You were there while the entire world – in their homes – were following you. Millions of television cameras were pointed toward you, toward Peter. All the journalists were silent, astonished, mute. The world, knowing you were in the Square, had stopped everything to watch you. And, looking at you, they were looking at Him. There on your knees, you were the bridge: it is not by chance that they call you *Pontiff*. Supreme Pontiff: much more, therefore, than the Brooklyn Bridge or the one they are building in Genoa. You are the Bridge-to-God. And while you were praying there, I saw Mary holding her hand on your head. This is what many grandmothers in the North of Italy do with their grandchildren before they leave the house: 'May the Madonna keep her hand on your head,' they say. It's as if to say: Go! I will be waiting for you on your return! God on High never seemed so close to you. Do you remember, in that dark moment, when you recounted that passage from *Deuteronomy* that you like so much: "*For what great nation is there that has gods so close to it as the Lord, our God, is to us whenever we call upon him?*" (Deuteronomy 4:7). Moses, in today's first reading, had struck the rock and water gushed forth, thus dispelling all doubts. We are at war here. Direct contact with God will save us, not live streaming. That is not enough anymore: we need you with your Pontifical and Firefighter gear ... I am certainly not the one to suggest to you what to do: the inspiration is guaranteed by God, by that God who more than once has entrusted His message through the faint voice of dreams. To those who say: '*Where is the Pope?!*' respond with your presence: you are the 'bridge' between heaven and earth, an earth that languishes – a world that has evolved, that languishes – while you, having come from the southern hemisphere, are showing us that this trial is leaving its mark on our flesh of the pain that people have been suffering for centuries. This sick earth needs to lift its eyes to Heaven and believe that it needs only God, that it needs to be converted to God!

A *Statio Orbis*, Pope Francis, nothing less. A universal *Statio Orbis*. You, alone, in *Saint Peter's Square*, while the entire world is deserted and people are holed up in their homes, terrified of the contagious virus. They themselves are contagious: both infectious and infected at the same time. Raise your voice, your prayer, your intercession: implore God to come to our aid! The trial caused by this contagious virus is opening many hearts and minds to God. You are the 'greatest' man on the Earth: the Vicar of Christ. *Stop the world, the entire Church, so that the world might raise its mind and heart to God!* I beg you, Holy Father. Do it quickly! You have the best equipment to extinguish this blaze."[3]

"A *Statio Orbis*," Father Marco wrote again a week later, "is not theological fiction, much less a whimsical proposal made by those who, to raise the bar, propose the unthinkable. ... Form is not formality, but rather the proposal of content, a prelude to what is hidden. It is shrouded in Mystery. In the figure of Peter the pinnacle of his word goes hand in hand with the sweeping significance of his gestures: word and gesture. When Peter performs a gesture, the same type of gesture I can perform, that gesture assumes a completely different value. The person who accomplishes it multiplies its power by ten. The same is true regarding his words: in a split second human speech is not human if it is pronounced by Peter. Therefore, Peter does not turn to us, therefore, with words that have not first been prayed over while kneeling down, meditated, pondered, weighed. A theology done kneeling down is the only theology possible. Why, then, a Statio Orbis directed to the entire world? Why is there the need to halt in the midst of a wild race? 'Why run if you do not know where you are going?' I read on the wall of a railway station. ... A Statio Orbis is a station: do you have an idea of the old train stations? Imagine this: someone requests the train to stop for a moment, to stop in the station of Saint Peter's, to make a connection with Christ. It is not losing time, but taking time: a pause within the flux of history, 'to take stock of the way things are going and to reinforce the troops to go forward toward the future. On that stop, the entire Christian world is symbolically engaged and present' (G. Marchesi, *Civiltà Cattolica*, 2000, q. 3607, p.173). When it happens that the Church has a *Statio Orbis* before the Eucharist: 'the world stops' before a small fragment of Bread, which for Christians, is Christ (and Christ is God), because only in Him are we saved. It is a bit like that that I imagine that a man, Peter, could ask that 'the world stop' before Christ so that the world might believe that only in God are we saved. What do you want me to say to you? It is like asking the world to be humble, something it lacks quite a bit, that 'I do not need God' that is revealing the modern form of atheism."[4]

I cited Father Marco's words in full because they explain well the beginning, the origin, the Spirit (with a capital "S") which inspired Pope Francis.

If this was the prologue, how the event unfolded (which was then broadcast through the Vatican Media's cameramen and photographers) was conceived by the Master of Pontifical Liturgical Celebrations, Monsignor Guido Marini.

The television production was simple, basic.[5] Six television cameras captured the empty square and the Pope's prayer – his entrance, walking through the rain, the crucifix that seemed to be weeping, the clouds in the heavens, the splashes of light, the Pope praying, the sound of the sirens breaking the silence, the entire world watching, the invisible cameramen and photographers.

Once again we touch on the invisible. I think that we could speak for hours about how the idea came about, about the production, the lights, the photography, about why the Square was chosen and not the Basilica, about why the Pope climbed the steps, about the relationship between the empty square and the hundreds of millions of people united in prayer, about the silence and the words. But that would risk losing the sense of what happened, of thinking that the same rules that apply to film, television, theater and Hollywood apply to the Church when it communicates. But Pope Francis has warned us that that is how we end up "taming Christ." In this way, it would no longer have been a testimony to what Christ was doing, but it would have been a communication of an idea about Christ – an idea owned and controlled by those who were organizing everything as a small enterprise.[6]

The truth is that March 27 was a mysterious and powerful moment of *chairos* around a simple prayer.

As Pope Francis stated regarding Peter and the Apostles, "The Apostles are not the protagonists of the *Acts of the Apostles*. The protagonist is the Holy Spirit. The Apostles recognize this and are the first to attest to it. ... The Apostles' experience is a paradigm that is always valid. It is enough to think how things freely happen in the *Acts of the Apostles*, without being forced. It is an experience, a human story in which the disciples always arrive secondarily, they always arrive after the Holy Spirit has operated. He prepares and works on hearts. He disrupts their plans. It is He who accompanies them, guides them and consoles them in all of the situations they find themselves living. ... It is useless to get upset. It is useless to organize things ourselves or to scream and shout. Gimmicks and strategies are useless. We need to ask to be able to repeat the experience today that brings you to say, 'we have decided, the Holy Spirit and us.'... Without the Holy Spirit, wanting to do mission becomes something else. ... Anyone who thinks they are the protagonist or manager of mission, with all the good intentions in the world and declarations of intent, often end up not attracting anyone. Mission is not ... a show organized to count how many people show up thanks to our promotional efforts. The Holy Spirit works as He wills, when He wills, and where He wills."[7]

The extraordinary quality of March 27 lies precisely here. Its communicative capacity arises from the truth. The Pope was alone like each one of us. We are all alone before God. We are all united before God. We are all weak and in His hands.

In one of his homilies delivered in the Casa Santa Marta Chapel, Pope Francis said: "The Lord always consoles with His *closeness*, through *truth* and *hope*. ... In *closeness*, never distant: I am here.

These beautiful words: I am here. I am here, with you. And very often, in silence. But we know that He is there. He is always there. That closeness that is God's style, even in the Incarnation, making Himself close to us. The Lord consoles in closeness. And He does not use empty words; on the contrary, He prefers silence. The strength of closeness, in presence. He speaks little, but He is close."[8]

The word always needs silence. And silence is eloquent only when the word echoes. Thus it was on March 27. That silence, as the Pope said, questioned us: *"Why are you afraid? Have you no faith?"* That silence was an appeal to believe – an urgent appeal: "Be converted!", "Return to me with all your heart" (*Jl* 2:12). That silence called us "to seize this time of trial as *a time of choosing*." In that silence Pope Francis's words resounded: "It is not the time of your judgment, but of our judgment: a time to choose what matters and what passes away, a time to separate what is necessary from what is not. It is a time to get our lives back on track with regard to You, Lord, and to others."

**Paolo Ruffini**

Prefect of the Dicastery for Communication

---

[1] Translator's note: The term *Statio Orbis*, was first used during the 37th Eucharistic Congress held in 1960 in Munich. It refers to the conclusion of international events in the Catholic Church in which people from all over the world participate at which either the Pope himself or his representative presides.

[2] MARCO POZZA, *A Sua Immagine*, RaiPlay, March 15, 2020, https://www.youtube.com/watch?v=v92a4NXWYAw

[3] MARCO POZZA, *Papa(') Francesco, in ginocchio: "Intervieni tu, fai presto"! (Pope Francis on his knees: "Intervene, do so quickly"!)*, March 15, 2020, https://www.sullastradadiemmaus.it/
sezioni-del-sito/ approfondimenti/3386-papa-francesco-inginocchio- intervieni -tu-fai-presto

[4] MARCO POZZA, *Il Papa annuncia la "Statio orbis" per il globo che vorrà (The Pope Announces the "Statio orbis" he Wants for the World)*, March 22, 2020, https://www.sullastradadiemmaus.it/
sezioni-del-sito/approfondimenti/3396-il-papa-annuncia la- statio orbis-per-il-globo-che-vorra

[5] Cfr. Dario Edoardo VIGANÒ, *Francesco: scena e drammatica dell'amore (Pope Francis: Dramatic and loving scene)*, *Settimana News*, April 19, 2020, http://www.settimananews.it/papa/francesco-scena-drammatica-amore/

[6] POPE FRANCIS, *Without Jesus we can do nothing*, Novalis, 2020. (translated from the Italian version: *Senza di Lui non possiamo far nulla*, LEV 2019, pp. 15-16).

[7] See *Without Jesus we can do nothing* (translated from the Italian version: pp. 21-30).

[8] POPE FRANCIS, *Homily*, Casa Santa Marta, May 8, 2020 - http://www.vatican.va/content/francesco/en/cotidie/2020/
documents/papa-francesco-cotidie_20200508_lavicinanza-lostile-didio.html

# The Holy Father's Meditation

**Sagrato of Saint Peter's Basilica**
March 27, 2020

# "When evening had come" (*Mk* 4:35)

The Gospel passage we have just heard begins like this.

For weeks now it has been evening.

Thick darkness has gathered over our squares, our streets and our cities; it has taken over our lives, filling everything with a deafening silence and a distressing void, that stops everything as it passes by; we feel it in the air, we notice in people's gestures, their glances give them away.

We find ourselves afraid and lost.

Like the disciples in the Gospel we were caught off guard by an unexpected, turbulent storm.

We have realized that we are on the same boat, all of us fragile and disoriented, but at the same time important and needed, all of us called to row together, each of us in need of comforting the other.

On this boat … are all of us.

Just like those disciples, who spoke anxiously with one voice, saying "We are perishing" (v. 38), so we too have realized that we cannot go on thinking of ourselves, but only together can we do this.

It is easy to recognize ourselves in this story.

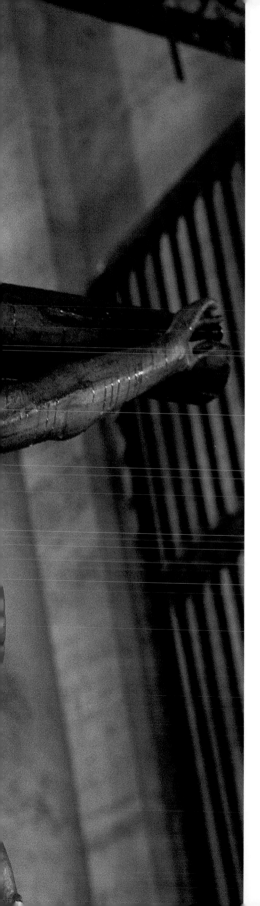

What is harder to understand is Jesus' attitude.

While his disciples are quite naturally alarmed and desperate, he is in the stern, in the part of the boat that sinks first.

And what does he do?

In spite of the tempest, he sleeps on soundly, trusting in the Father; this is the only time in the Gospels we see Jesus sleeping.

When he wakes up, after calming the wind and the waters, he turns to the disciples in a reproaching voice: "Why are you afraid? Have you no faith?" (v. 40).

Let us try to understand.

In what does the lack of the disciples' faith consist,
as contrasted with Jesus' trust?

They had not stopped believing in him; in fact, they
called on him.

But we see how they call on him: "Teacher, do you not
care if we perish?" (v. 38).

*Do you not care*: they think that Jesus is not interested in them,
does not care about them.

One of the things that hurts us and our families most when we
hear it said is: "Do you not care about me?"

It is a phrase that wounds and unleashes storms in our hearts.
It would have shaken Jesus too.

Because he, more than anyone, cares about us. Indeed, once
they have called on him, he saves his disciples from their
discouragement.

The storm exposes our vulnerability and uncovers those false
and superfluous certainties around which we have constructed
our daily schedules, our projects, our habits and priorities.

It shows us how we have allowed to become dull and feeble the very things that nourish, sustain and strengthen our lives and our communities.

The tempest lays bare all our prepackaged ideas and forgetfulness of what nourishes our people's souls; all those attempts that anesthetize us with ways of thinking and acting that supposedly "save" us, but instead prove incapable of putting us in touch with our roots and keeping alive the memory of those who have gone before us. We deprive ourselves of the antibodies we need to confront adversity.

In this storm, the façade of those stereotypes with which we camouflaged our egos, always worrying about our image, has fallen away, uncovering once more that (blessed) common belonging, of which we cannot be deprived: our belonging as brothers and sisters.

*"Why are you afraid? Have you no faith?"*

Lord, your word this evening strikes us and regards us,
all of us.

In this world, that you love more than we do, we have gone
ahead at breakneck speed, feeling powerful and able to do
anything.

Greedy for profit, we let ourselves get caught up in things,
and lured away by haste.

We did not stop at your reproach to us, we were not shaken
awake by wars or injustice across the world, nor did we listen
to the cry of the poor or of our ailing planet.

We carried on regardless, thinking we would stay healthy
in a world that was sick.

Now that we are in a stormy sea, we implore you:
"Wake up, Lord!"

*"Why are you afraid? Have you no faith?"*

Lord, you are calling to us, calling us to faith. Which is not so much believing that you exist, but coming to you and trusting in you.

This Lent your call reverberates urgently: "Be converted!", "Return to me with all your heart" (*Jl* 2:12).

You are calling on us to seize this time of trial as a *time of choosing*.

It is not the time of your judgment, but of our judgment: a time to choose what matters and what passes away, a time to separate what is necessary from what is not.

It is a time to get our lives back on track with regard to you, Lord, and to others.

We can look to so many exemplary companions for the journey, who, even though fearful, have reacted by giving their lives.

This is the force of the Spirit poured out and fashioned in courageous and generous self-denial. It is the life in the Spirit that can redeem, value and demonstrate how our lives are woven together and sustained by ordinary people – often forgotten people – who do not appear in newspaper and magazine headlines nor on the grand catwalks of the latest show, but who without any doubt are in these very days writing the decisive events of our time: doctors, nurses, supermarket employees, cleaners, caregivers, providers of transport, law and order forces, volunteers, priests, religious men and women and so very many others who have understood that no one reaches salvation by themselves.

In the face of so much suffering, where the authentic development of our peoples is assessed, we experience the priestly prayer of Jesus: "That they may all be one" (*Jn* 17:21).

How many people every day are exercising patience and offering hope, taking care to sow not panic but a shared responsibility. How many fathers, mothers, grandparents and teachers are showing our children, in small everyday gestures, how to face up to and navigate a crisis by adjusting their routines, lifting their gaze and fostering prayer. How many are praying, offering and interceding for the good of all. Prayer and quiet service: these are our victorious weapons.

*"Why are you afraid? Have you no faith?"*

Faith begins when we realize we are in need of salvation.

We are not self-sufficient; by ourselves we founder:
We need the Lord, like ancient navigators needed the stars.
Let us invite Jesus into the boats of our lives.

Let us hand over our fears to him so that he can
conquer them.

Like the disciples, we will experience that with him
on board there will be no shipwreck.

Because this is God's strength: turning to the good
everything that happens to us, even the bad things.
He brings serenity into our storms, because with
God life never dies.

The Lord asks us and, in the midst of our tempest, invites us to reawaken and put into practice that solidarity and hope capable of giving strength, support and meaning to these hours when everything seems to be floundering.

The Lord awakens so as to reawaken and revive our Easter faith.

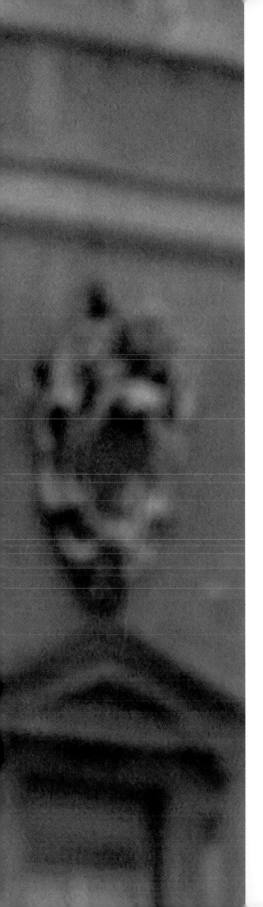

We have an anchor: By his cross we have been saved.

We have a rudder: By his cross we have been redeemed.

We have a hope: by his cross we have been healed and embraced so that nothing and no one can separate us from his redeeming love.

In the midst of isolation when we are suffering from a lack of tenderness and chances to meet up, and we experience the loss of so many things, let us once again listen to the proclamation that saves us: he is risen and is living by our side.

The Lord asks us from his cross to rediscover the life that awaits us, to look towards those who look to us, to strengthen, recognize and foster the grace that lives within us. Let us not quench the wavering flame (see *Is* 42:3) that never falters, and let us allow hope to be rekindled.

Embracing his cross means finding the courage to embrace all the hardships of the present time, abandoning for a moment our eagerness for power and possessions in order to make room for the creativity that only the Spirit is capable of inspiring.

It means finding the courage to create spaces where everyone can recognize that they are called, and to allow new forms of hospitality, fraternity and solidarity.

By his cross we have been saved in order to embrace hope and let it strengthen and sustain all measures and all possible avenues for helping us protect ourselves and others. Embracing the Lord in order to embrace hope: that is the strength of faith, which frees us from fear and gives us hope.

*"Why are you afraid? Have you no faith?"*

Dear brothers and sisters, from this place that tells of Peter's rock-solid faith, I would like this evening to entrust all of you to the Lord, through the intercession of Mary, Health of the People and Star of the stormy Sea.

From this colonnade that embraces Rome and the whole world, may God's blessing come down upon you as a consoling embrace.

Lord, may you bless the world, give health to our bodies and comfort our hearts. You ask us not to be afraid. Yet our faith is weak and we are fearful. But you, Lord, will not leave us at the mercy of the storm. Tell us again, "Do not be afraid" (*Mt* 28:5). And we, together with Peter, "cast all our anxieties onto you, for you care about us" (see *1 Pt* 5:7).

# Memories of a prayer
# that united the world

The Pope has just finished one of his Wednesday audiences.

He is wrapped in silence and is watching the images from March 27, reliving what happened on that Friday of Lent. He is retracing that *Statio Orbis* celebrated in an empty Saint Peter's Square, under the rain, the prayers interrupted by the sound of the sirens. It is more than an experience of merely remembering what happened. His face reflects the fact that he is praying.

We ask him what he was feeling while he silently ascended the sagrato of the Basilica:

**"I was walking like that, alone, thinking about the solitude of so many people ... a thought that included everyone, a thought from my head and my heart together ... I was feeling all that while I was walking ..."**

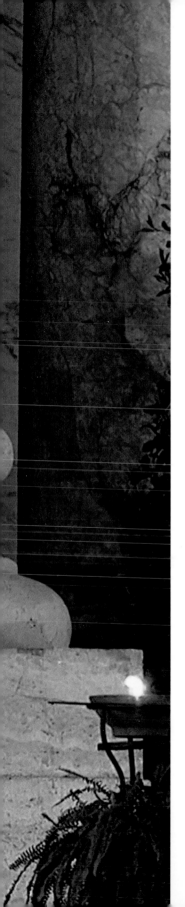

The world was watching the Bishop of Rome and was praying with him, in silence. It was watching the Pope as an intercessor between God and us, His people. So, we ask Pope Francis what he said to God in those moments:

**"You know this, you already resolved a situation like this in the 1500s, '*meté mano*.'[1] This expression, 'put your hand' is really mine. Many times, in prayer, I say: 'Put your hands on us, please!'"**

[1] "*Meté mano*" is a slang expression in Spanish. It is colloquial, informal and popular, widely used in Argentina, especially in Buenos Aires.

The Pope's eyes linger on the empty Saint Peter's Square.
We ask him what he was thinking at that moment, what his
thoughts were about the people and the suffering of so many people:

**"Two things were going through my mind: the empty square,
people united at a distance ... and from this side, the boat with
migrants, that monument. ... And we are all in the boat, and in this
boat we do not know how many will be able to land. ... The whole
drama is in front of the boat, the plague, the loneliness ... in silence ..."**

The boat is cited in the Gospel of Mark which was read that
evening. And it is present in the square, depicted in the monument
that memorializes migrants. This is why every now and then, the
Bishop of Rome's gaze turned toward the colonnade on the right,
toward that barely distinguishable monument in the obscurity.

**"The boat! ..."** the Pope repeats, almost whispering.

So, we ask what he was thinking about in particular during those
moments, who he felt were most in need, who he was entrusting to
the Lord during that prayer. He responds once again, in a low voice:

**"Everything was united: the people, the boat and everyone's
suffering ..."**

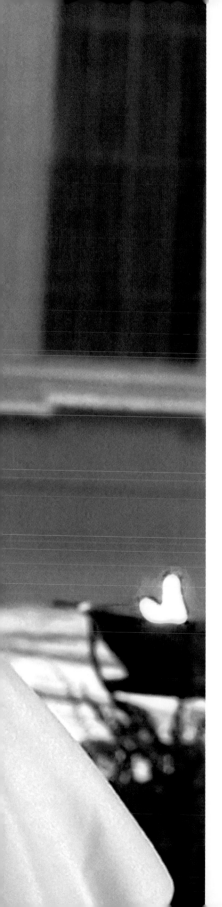

What was sustaining the Pope?
What was giving him strength and hope in such an intense and dramatic moment?
Pope Francis remains in silence a few moments, looking at the images:

**"Kissing the feet of the Crucified Christ always gives hope. He knows what it means to walk and He knows all about quarantine because they put two nails there to keep Him there. Jesus' feet are a compass for people's lives, when to walk and when to stand still. The Lord's feet are very touching for me ..."**

The images continue scrolling slowly.
Then the one appears that shows him with the liturgical vestments in the atrium of the Basilica. On the pavement is a large engraved inscription, *11 October 1962*. We bring this to his attention.
Right away, he exclaims:

**"It was the beginning of the Council!"**

We remind him of the citation of Pope John XXIII's famous "Moon Discourse" when he unexpectedly came to the window of his study to bless the large crowd of the faithful holding candles and said: "Bring the Pope's hug to your children."[2]
Pope Francis listens silently ...

**"I didn't notice it at that moment ..."**

It is a coincidence ... almost as if to say that a new hug from the Pope needed to be brought to every home, within the suffering and loneliness of isolated families, to hospital wards where the sick were ascending their own Calvaries without the presence or comfort of their dear ones.

He nods his head: **"Yes ... yes ..."**

[2] *"Returning home, you will find your children; give them a hug and say: 'This is a hug from the Pope'. You will find some tears to dry. Do something, say a good word. The Pope is with you especially in the sad and bitter moments"* (Saint John XXIII).

http://www.vatican.va/content/john-xxiii/it/speeches/1962/documents/hf_j-xxiii_spe_19621011_luna.html

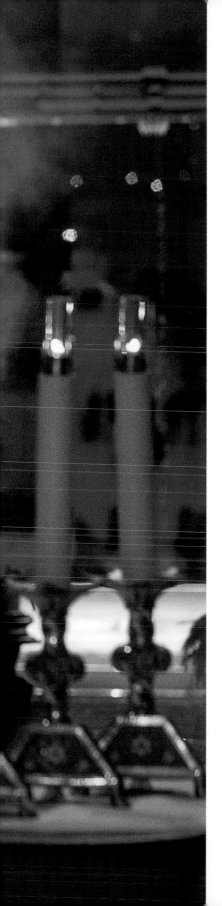

We ask him to continue remembering, to think once again about those moments as he views the images captured at the time.

**"I was in prayer before the Lord ... there ...**

**An intercessory prayer before God ..."**

The absence of people in the desolately empty square is striking. It was so different than all the other times, than all the other celebrations. But did the Pope sense the presence of the faithful, of believers and unbelievers? Was he aware of the many people who were connected at that moment with the Successor of Peter and with themselves through the media?

**"I was in contact with the people. There was no moment in which I was alone ..."**

But about the empty square, he adds:

**"... it was quite impressive."**

The *Statio Orbis* was so sparse, devoid of everything.
The presence of the people of God was missing. But there were some meaningful types of presence. We ask him about what he experienced:

**"Well. The Virgin was there ...
I myself asked if the Virgin could be there, the *Salus Populi romani*, I wanted her to be there ... And Christ,
... The Miraculous Christ ..."**

Some people have said and have written that March 27 was an event destined to remain in the annals of history and in everyone's memory.
The Pope closes the book on his memories, concluding:

**It was something original ...**
**It all began because of a poor prison chaplain ..."**

Compiled by **Lucio Adrián Ruiz**

# The Rite

## I. Welcomed by the Word of God

**The Holy Father:**

In the name of the Father and of the Son and of the Holy Spirit.
> **R/. Amen.**

Let us pray.
Almighty and merciful God,
behold our sorrowful condition:
comfort your children and open our hearts to hope,
so that we might feel
your Fatherly presence in our midst.
Through our Lord Jesus Christ, your Son,
Who lives and reigns with You in the unity of the Holy Spirit, one God,
for ever and ever.
> **R/. Amen.**

## Gospel

Listen to the Word of the Lord from the Gospel According to Mark (4, 35-41)

On that day, as evening drew on, he said to them, "Let us cross to the other side." Leaving the crowd, they took him with them in the boat just as he was. And other boats were with him. A violent squall came up and waves were breaking over the boat, so that it was already filling up. Jesus was in the stern, asleep on a cushion. They woke him and said to him, "Teacher, do you not care that we are perishing?" He woke up, rebuked the wind, and said to the sea, "Quiet! Be still!"

The wind ceased and there was great calm. Then he asked them, "Why are you terrified? Do you not yet have faith?" They were filled with great awe and said to one another, "Who then is this whom even wind and sea obey?"

# The Holy Father's discourse

# II. Exposition, Adoration and Benediction of the Blessed Sacrament

## Litany of Supplication

We adore you, O Lord

True God and true man, truly present in this holy Sacrament.
    **R/. We adore you, O Lord**
Our Savior, God with us, faithful and rich in mercy
    **R/. We adore you, O Lord**
King and Lord of creation and of history
    **R/. We adore you, O Lord**
Conqueror of sin and death
    **R/. We adore you, O Lord**
Friend of humankind, the Risen One, the Living One who sits at the right hand of the Father.
    **R/. We adore you, O Lord**

We believe in you, O Lord

Only begotten Son of the Father, descended from heaven for our salvation
    **R/. We believe in you, O Lord**
Heavenly physician, who bows down over our misery
    **R/. We believe in you, O Lord**
Lamb who was slain, who offer yourself to rescue us from evil
    **R/. We believe in you, O Lord**
Good Shepherd, who give your life for the flock which you love
    **R/. We believe in you, O Lord**
Living bread and medicine for immortality, who give us eternal life
    **R/. We believe in you, O Lord**

Deliver us, O Lord

From the power of Satan and the seductions of the world
**R/. Deliver us, O Lord**
From the pride and presumption of being able to do anything without you
**R/. Deliver us, O Lord**
From the deceptions of fear and anxiety
**R/. Deliver us, O Lord**
From unbelief and desperation
**R/. Deliver us, O Lord**
From hardness of heart and the incapacity to love
**R/. Deliver us, O Lord**

Save us, O Lord

From every evil that afflicts humanity
**R/. Save us, O Lord**
From hunger, from famine and from egoism
**R/. Save us, O Lord**
From illnesses, epidemics and the fear of our brothers and sisters
**R/. Save us, O Lord**
From devastating madness, from ruthless interests and from violence
**R/. Save us, O Lord**
From being deceived, from false information and the manipulation of consciences
**R/. Save us, O Lord**

Comfort us, O Lord

Protect your Church which crosses the desert
**R/. Comfort us, O Lord**
Protect humanity terrified by fear and anguish
**R/. Comfort us, O Lord**
Protect the sick and the dying, oppressed by loneliness
**R/. Comfort us, O Lord**
Protect doctors and healthcare providers exhausted by the difficulties they are facing
**R/. Comfort us, O Lord**
Protect politicians and decision makers who bear the weight of having to make decisions
**R/. Comfort us, O Lord**

Grant us your Spirit, O Lord

In the hour of trial and from confusion
 **R/. Grant us your Spirit, O Lord**
In temptation and in our fragility
 **R/. Grant us your Spirit, O Lord**
In the battle against evil and sin
 **R/. Grant us your Spirit, O Lord**
In the search for what is truly good and true joy
 **R/. Grant us your Spirit, O Lord**
In the decision to remain in you and in your friendship
 **R/. Grant us your Spirit, O Lord**

Open us to hope, O Lord

Should sin oppress us
 **R/. Open us to hope, O Lord**
Should hatred close our hearts
 **R/. Open us to hope, O Lord**
Should sorrow visit us
 **R/. Open us to hope, O Lord**
Should indifference cause us anguish
 **R/. Open us to hope, O Lord**
Should death overwhelm us
 **R/. Open us to hope, O Lord**

## Benediction of the Blessed Sacrament

**The Holy Father:**

Let us pray:
O God,
who in this wonderful Sacrament
have left us a memorial of your Passion,
grant us, we pray, so to revere

the sacred mysteries of your Body and Blood
that we may always experience in ourselves the fruits of your redemption.
Who live and reign with God the Father in the unity of the Holy Spirit, on God, for ever and ever.
**R/. Amen.**

## Announcement of the indulgence

### The Cardinal

His Holiness Pope Francis grants a ple¬nary indulgence in the form laid down by the Church
to all the faithful who receive this Eucharistic Benediction, either through the various
communications technologies, or by uniting themselves spiritually and by desire, to the
present rite:

**The Holy Father gives the benediction with the Blessed Sacrament.**

## Divine Praises

- Blessed be God.
- Blessed be His Holy Name.
- Blessed be Jesus Christ, true God and true Man.
- Blessed be the Name of Jesus.
- Blessed be His Most Sacred Heart.
- Blessed be His Most Precious Blood.
- Blessed be Jesus in the Most Holy Sacrament of the Altar.
- Blessed be the Holy Spirit, the Paraclete.
- Blessed be the great Mother of God, Mary most Holy.
- Blessed be her Holy and Immaculate Conception.
- Blessed be her Glorious Assumption.
- Blessed be the name of Mary, Virgin and Mother.
- Blessed be St. Joseph, her most chaste spouse.
- Blessed be God in His Angels and in His Saints.

# Conclusion

## Part I

"That you may tell your children and grandchildren." (*Exodus* 10:2)

The celebration of March 27 will remain etched in the memories of all men and women who, locked down, frightened and lost due to the unexpected tempest of the Covid-19 pandemic, were watching Pope Francis from the heart of the Church on their screens. Breathing heavily, he went up to the Temple and bade us to wake up. He made Jesus' words resound in almost every corner of the universe: "*Why are you afraid? Have you no faith?*" He reminded us that we are sinking alone and he invited us to surrender our fears to Jesus, and through Him, to obtain serenity in the midst of the tempest. Then he entrusted everyone to the Lord, through the intercession of Mary, Protectress of His People. He prayed to God in silence, at the foot of the cross of Christ, and he blessed us with the Blessed Sacrament ...

This story we are narrating, *that you may tell your children and grandchildren*, took place at the height of the Covid-19 tragedy which affected all of humanity, bringing with it loneliness, fear, sickness and death. This is the story of a unique event that touched and enfolded all of humanity.

It was a highly original liturgical act because it was a celebration that *reflected history* and *became history*:

- It *reflected history* because it presented the human tragedy to the God of Mercy.

- It *became history* because God's response was *His Presence*, present in the midst of His People, a presence that blesses and accompanies.

Translated into liturgical language, this double movement was reflected in a web of signs, words and events that manifested the suffering of humanity that was waiting for something, but which needed to be called and exhorted toward faith and trust on the one hand, and on the other hand, to remember God's unfailing faithfulness who, in the midst of humanity, blesses everyone to strengthen and accompany them so as to guide them along the trajectory of history.

Parallel to the liturgy that unfolded in an organized, simple and essential context that framed the celebration, there was also an aspect that was not prepared, elements that contributed to the creation of a rich and profound narrative and provoke memories and emotion, make us recall other events, and make us remember what is essential.

That historic moment was characterized by the fact that the quarantine prevented the participation of the faithful. For this reason, for the first time in history, a Pope celebrated an *Urbi et Orbi* in a deserted Square, without the People of God present. On the other hand, connecting the faith, life and the culture in which we live which has been transformed by the *virtuality* of relationships and activities – which so often had been difficult for us to reconcile with spirituality – that day, paradoxically, we discovered that it was precisely that *virtuality* that "filled" Saint Peter's Square like no other moment, with pilgrims "participating virtually" from every corner of the globe.

That celebration thus became an event marking the world's journey of faith and hope. It is an event that has remained impressed on the minds and hearts not only of believers, but of all those who, in some way, seeking an explanation of the phenomenon in the least bit credible for the contemporary world, found not only a response in that liturgy, but also a hope that struck the heart because of its intensity, because it evoked something much greater and larger – the story of the love, the faithfulness and the presence of God in the midst of humanity.

This is why it is important, as we read the Holy Father's Message for the World Day of Communications 2020, to read this event in the light of *history*: so that, as the theme says, "*you may tell your children and grandchildren.*" This is necessary so that in this way, *life becomes history*, history that is remembered, history that is relived, history that is handed down to future generations, so that they might take part in the great story of God's journey with humanity. The present moment is not only marked by this virus, but it is fundamentally sealed by God's Presence. This is what needs to be remembered and recounted *to our children and grandchildren* so it becomes part of the collective memory. ...

The event was not intended to show something, *to be seen*, as much as to create an event *to be experienced*. It was meant to *enter* into homes in order to *enter* into hearts. So, even though the square was not filled with bodies, paradoxically, it was the people who were filled spiritually, who were helped *virtually* to experience, to be united to the mystery that was being celebrated.

A narrative is not that of a writer or artist who retreats into silence to invoke inspiration from a muse in order to conceive an idea to write about and to weave the plot of his or her story. A narrative is that of the "shepherd with the smell of the sheep," that of the intercessor who puts himself between God, whose name is Mercy, and the People for whom the Son gave His life and who now implores that Mercy.

Therefore, the narrative of this event wove the plot between the Merciful God always present in human history, and His Church who, *filled with fear*, interceded for those who needed to be encouraged to believe and trust once again in the certain presence of God. In short, it was not a narrative other than the many others found in Sacred Scripture, with the exception that this one unfolded within the context of a liturgical celebration in the Vatican, in today's globalized world, with a global pandemic in full swing.

Yes, it was born from silence, but from a contemplative silence, one that enters into the mystery of God and the mystery of human suffering. This is no inspiring muse, but the exercise of the Papal ministry, one that builds a bridge between God and humanity.

But it was not born from silence alone. It was born also from the Pope's shared experience of suffering with the Church which he guides as its Bishop and Shepherd and of which he is also a member, insofar as he is a Christian. This theological and spiritual reality is reflected in the moving image of the Holy Father's presence in the Square, a place where people gather, a Temple, a place where God is present. This was implicitly communicated in that procession bringing the People of God with him, representing them in that unique movement toward that place of contemplation and that blessed presence.

It is, therefore, from the point of view of a Pastor and Intercessor that the basic narrative is understood. This presupposes an awareness of God's Merciful Love so as to intercede, of humanity's need so as to know what to ask for, and also the knowledge of how to exhort the Church to awaken its faith, trust and hope because the faithful God asks for fidelity.

*"Why are you afraid? Have you no faith?"*

Jesus' question is a tremendous admonition: *"Why are you afraid? Have you no faith?"* This is the common thread not only of his homily, but of the entire event, for the prior ascending represented the "coming out of the world of fear" out of which rises the question: *"Why are you afraid?"*; and the benediction with the Blessed Sacrament represented the clear presence of Jesus in History, and thus the question: *"Have you no faith?"* So, the two questions, *"Why are you afraid?"* and *"Have you no faith?"* are the refrain, the link, the axis, the beginning and the end of the event because giving certainty about the promise *"I am with you always, even to the end of time"* is the key for not being afraid and for remaining solid in the faith. With Jesus on board the boat of History, it will not sink. Thus, just as Jesus woke up to revive the faith of the disciples, the Holy Father went up to the Temple to revive the faith of the contemporary world.

A particular element regarding that act of "bringing humanity to the Temple" was a way of drawing attention to all the "ordinary people – often forgotten people – who do not appear in newspaper and magazine headlines ... but who without any doubt are in these very days writing the decisive events of our time." Everyone can be found among them, beginning with the least, those on the "existential peripheries."

The call to seek Jesus as disciples, to hope and believe in Him, was clear and not sugar-coated, and situated within a correct Christological dimension: "We have an anchor: by His cross we have been saved. We have a rudder: by His cross we have been redeemed. We have a hope: by His cross we have been healed and embraced so that nothing and no one can separate us from His redeeming love." Thus, "now that we are in a stormy sea," with the same hope the disciples had, "we implore you: 'Wake up, Lord!'"

## The awaited Miracle

"*Do you not care?*" the disciples asked, just as we ask God many times in our lives: *Don't you care about our sufferings? Why are you silent? Why are you sleeping?* ...

We need to draw near to Jesus for the response, we need to return to Him because He alone can calm the tempest and calm the waters.

Many anxiously participated in that prayer seeking some "miracle." The Gospel chosen for the event seemed to follow that line – as if the event had been planned so that the hoped-for miracle might happen, like the sea calmed by Jesus, that the virus would disappear with the Benediction. Just like that, in an instant, miracle accomplished, no more virus, everyone happy – and then the next day, as the frenetic *routine* of a "sick world" returned, it would all seem like a nightmare with a happy ending.

And then – and it would not be the first time – we would have forgotten the great miracle, we would have left it in the past. ... In the Gospel we find so many of these types of accounts: great miracles that the people did not understand and which, no one remembered anymore along the Way of the Cross. It's enough to think of what happened after the multiplication of the loaves and fish.

The meaning of Jesus' miracles lies not in the miracles themselves, but in the sign that He wanted to give and in what it meant: to restore sight to a blind person was a way of saying, "I am the Light of the world"; to feed people till they were satisfied was a way of saying, "I am the Bread of Life"; to raise a dead person was a way of saying, "I am the Life." For Jesus, the event was not the miracle but the message that it contained. Above all, the true miracle was not the healing or the multiplication of the loaves, but that the disciples came to believe. Faith in Jesus is the miracle because faith is essential for Salvation: "The one who believes in me has life eternal." The object of the miracle is faith: "That they might believe" (see *Jn* 16).

In fact, the miracles that bore fruit were those that led the disciples to a confession of faith and to follow the Lord, as happened with the man who was blind from birth. His story demonstrates a marvelous confession of faith: "Who is he so that I may believe? ... Yes, I do believe" (see *Jn* 9:1–41).

The miracles "lacking" in peoples' hearts are those which lead many to limit themselves to the material level, to the event itself: He multiplied bread, and they wanted to make Him king so that He might give them bread without having to work for it. Events that, in the majority of cases, do not lead to faith in God's presence, do not produce a movement toward faith, but are rather a request for a completely human stability, a simplification of how needs are satisfied or how problems are resolved.

For some, this human impulse could have been the same regarding the *Statio Orbis*: looking for a "magical" event to resolve the problem, to bring an end to the suffering and to return to life as usual.

So, in the eyes of many "nothing happened": the hoped-for miracle did not take place.

But in reality, if we look at it with Jesus' eyes, the miracle happened, because the goal was to *animate the faith of believers, to awaken their hearts to hope and to promote creative charity* so that Love might be manifested in the world.

"Behold, I make all things new." (*Revelation* 21:5)

If the event was not a television show, neither was it a work of "magic" to ward off the virus, or a "devout celebration" detached from the world and from history, thus remaining stuck. As the disciples gazing into the heavens after the Lord's Ascension, so we too, Christians and all men and women of goodwill, cannot remain immobile at the memory of that special celebration. The *Statio Orbis,* and the entire prayer itself, should be the point of departure to create something new, for a radical cultural shift, for a new beginning, for a new future.

The *Statio Orbis* was not a prayer for God's Mercy but it was an exhortation to the People to create a new life, a new history. Thus, from the meditation he provided in this liturgy a Papal Magisterium begins, a teaching that provides a rich analysis of the reality and its causes – how humanity has contributed to the manifestation of the crisis, and therefore, the need for a change of life. If the pandemic has manifested the weakness of our culture and of our way of living in society and in our *common home*, it is necessary that we learn from the crisis how to emerge from it different, because *you never come out of a crisis the same: you are either better or worse after it, but never the same.*

To be able to understand and allow ourselves to be enlightened by the nourishing Magisterium that follows from this event, in the *Second Part* of this book, we have gathered the main discourses of the Holy Father in which he explains *in a nutshell* what he said during the *Statio Orbis* Meditation.

**Lucio Adrián Ruiz**

# What We Need to Learn from the Pandemic

## The Magisterium of Pope Francis

# Introduction

## Part II

Pope Francis's Magisterium became richer after March 27. A common thread connects each homily, message, meditation ... to accompany the world with an illuminating analysis of the situation, encouraging creative action and instilling that hope that comes from the Crucified and Risen One. His Magisterium invites us to consider this historical reality as a moment of Grace to reconsider our life, to question ourselves about what our culture has become, what our relationships with others have been reduced to and how everyone is treating our common home. Not to welcome this Grace would be to waste this moment and, with it, the pain and suffering of all of humanity.

On **April 12**, Easter Sunday, the Holy Father initiated a string of messages that have accompanied our lives during this time of the pandemic. They have not ended, just as neither our suffering nor the worldwide crisis have ended. His teaching accompanies the daily routine of our lives while we weep for our dead and recover our health – not only our own health, but that of our *sick world* as well: "Christ is Risen!" Pope Francis exclaimed in his *Urbi et Orbi* message, and he called us to begin another "contagion," one that is heart-to-heart, a contagion of love and hope. The Risen One bursts in even though the doors have been locked; He appears at a "bad moment" when the community is locked in, confused, filled with fear. The experience of the Resurrection is not a point of arrival, but of departure, it is a beginning, a sending-forth.

On **April 17**, the Pope described in the periodical *Vida Nueva* a "plan to rise again." Inviting people to be joyful, Pope Francis wrote, might seem provoking, even a bad joke considering the consequences of Covid-19. And yet, before doubt, suffering, perplexity and even before fear, the Pope calls us to assume the attitude of the women of the Gospel who witnessed to the resurrection. "Behold, I am doing something new! Now it springs forth, do you not perceive it?" (*Is* 43:19). This is the right moment to encourage us to adopt a new imagination, to allow ourselves to be guided by the Spirit so as to "make all things new" (*Rv* 21:5).

During his homily for Holy Mass on Divine Mercy Sunday, **April 19**, the Holy Father warned us about a more dangerous virus, "*selfish indifference* which is spread by the thought that life is better if it is better for me." The antidote is that "mercy that does not abandon those who are left behind."

On **May 30**, the Vigil of Pentecost, Pope Francis stated once again that "no one is saved alone," "we are a single humanity" in need of the Spirit to give us new eyes, to open our minds and our hearts. His words seem to be a preview of his forthcoming encyclical. "When we come out of this pandemic, we will no longer be able to do what we have been doing, how we have been doing it": There are other pandemics to uproot, such as poverty. We will either be *better or worse* after, *but never the same.*

Pope Francis addressed a letter to all the priests of Rome on **May 31** to share with all of them what he had been thinking and feeling during the pandemic. In that letter, he recognizes the difficulty of finding the way forward, as well as the mission of keeping hope alive and of working for a new "normal" which "will either be completely new, or something much worse than what we have been used to."

On **September 25**, Pope Francis addressed the General Assembly of the United Nations (which had already recognized the gravity of the Covid-19 pandemic) with a call to choose between what really counts and what is passing, to separate what is necessary from what is not. He pointed out to the Assembly the unique opportunity to convert, of transformation, to reconsider our life styles and our economic and social systems. He ended up indicating the greatest truth that the pandemic is showing us: "we cannot live without one another, or worse still, pitted against one another."

Pope Francis signed his third Encyclical, *Fratelli tutti*, on **October 3** in Assisi, in front of Saint Francis's tomb. We are all sisters and brothers. The pandemic, the Pope says "unexpectedly erupted" while he was writing the Encyclical. His wish is that God might grant that in the end there will not be "others" any more, but only "us." The pandemic has proven the fragility of world systems.

Prior to announcing the publication of his Encyclical, over the course of nine General Audiences (**from August 5 to September 30**), Pope Francis offered a series of catechesis entitled: *Healing the World* through the transformation of the roots of our physical, spiritual and social maladies.

**Introduction (August 5)**: How can we contribute to the healing of our world today? While the prevention and the cure of the pandemic lies within the competence of people who have the civil and political responsibility, through the ages, the Church has developed several fundamental social principles in the light of the Gospel, which are expressed in the Compendium of the Social Doctrine of the Church, each of which offers the possibility of healing one of the world's great maladies.

**Faith and human dignity (August 12)**: When considering the pathology of the distorted vision or blindness that ignores the human person's dignity and relational character, reducing them to objects, it is necessary to renew that vision so it is capable of recognizing the human being as the bearer of an inalienable dignity. This means they must be recognized as brothers and sisters, never as strangers, looking on them with compassion and empathy. Let us ask God to "restore our sight":

with that new vision we must initiate concrete actions of compassion and respect for every person and of care and safeguarding of our common home.

**The preferential option for the poor and the virtue of charity (August 19):** The pandemic has exposed the plight of the poor and the great inequality that exists in the world. The preferential option for the poor cannot be lacking as a response because it is at the center of the Gospel, and is an essential criterion of authentic Christianity. It means walking together with them, letting ourselves be evangelized by them. We have the opportunity to build something different that will transform the roots of poverty. Let us ask the Lord to help us and give us the strength to be better after the pandemic, responding to the needs of today's world.

**The universal destination of goods and the virtue of love (August 26):** We risk losing hope. We have a sick economy due to unjust economic growth that disregards fundamental human values and does not care for our common home. The sin of wanting to possess and dominate our brothers and sisters, nature and even God Himself is the root. The earth "was here before us and it has been given to us," we are administrators, not masters, we have the duty to make sure that the earth's benefits are distributed to everyone, not only to a few. We must ask together, in Christian hope, rooted in God that He move our will to share, because this is the mission as disciples of Christ.

**Solidarity and the virtue of faith (September 2):** We are all connected to each other. To emerge from this crisis better than before, we have to do so together, in solidarity. Solidarity is not merely a question of helping others, it is a matter of justice. Each one of us is an instrument of Pentecost participating fully in the construction of the community at large. In the midst of crises and tempests, the Lord calls us and invites us to reawaken and activate this solidarity capable of giving solidity, support and meaning to these hours in which everything seems to be wrecked.

**Love and the common good (September):** The Christian response to the pandemic and the consequent crisis is based on love of God. True love that makes us fruitful and free is always expansive and inclusive, it heals and does good. It comprises civil and political relationships, including the relationship with nature. One of the highest expressions of love is specifically social and political. Inclusive love is social, familial, and political. Solutions for the pandemic must not bear traces of egoism, but must be built on the rock of the common good. Good politics are needed in order to improve our social love.

**Care of the common home and the contemplative dimension (September 16):** To emerge from a pandemic, we need to look after and care for each other and our common home. Abuse makes us sick: the best antidote to the misuse of our common home is contemplation. We need to be silent; we need to listen; we need to contemplate. Contemplation also heals the soul. When we contemplate, we discover in others and in nature something much greater than their usefulness. Contemplating is going beyond the usefulness of something. It is free. It leads to an attitude of care, it makes us more than spectators or protagonists. Those who cannot contemplate nature and creation cannot contemplate people in their true wealth. Those who know how to contemplate will more easily set to work to change what produces degradation. The contemplative in action tends to become a guardian of the environment. Contemplating and caring are two ways to correct, re-balance and heal our relationship with creation.

**Subsidiarity and the virtue of hope (September 23)**: The current crisis is at the same time a health crisis as well as a social, political and economic crisis. Each one of us is called to assume responsibility for our own part, that is, to share the responsibility. We must respond not only as individual people, but also as a society, from our principles and from our faith in God. So that there might be a true social reconstruction, we need the principle of subsidiarity that makes us more united; the collaboration among those on the top to those on the bottom and vice versa. Everyone needs to have the possibility of assuming their own responsibility in the healing processes of the society of which they are a part. There is no true solidarity without social participation. We must build a future where the local and global dimensions mutually enrich each other.

**Preparing the future together with Jesus who saves and heals (September 30)**: We are called to heal the world that suffers from an illness that the pandemic has highlighted and accentuated. We are called to walk together, keeping our eyes fixed on Jesus who saves and heals the world. In this world, we can regenerate society so as not to return to the sick "normal" from before the pandemic. The normality to which we are called is that of the Kingdom of God, where no one passes by looking the other way, where social organization is based on contributing and sharing. Tenderness, a sign of Jesus' presence, consists in drawing near to our neighbor to walk together, to heal and to help.

The Holy Father's call in this journey is that of reflecting and working together, as followers of Jesus who heal, so as to build a better world filled with hope: to heal the world, to free ourselves from the threats of dangerous viruses, to overcome the painful wounds inflicted by Covid-19 on humanity.

This will only be possible by recognizing that no one is saved alone because we are all brothers and sisters.

Therefore, in this second part, we present this little compendium of Pope Francis's principal teachings regarding the Covid-19 period, after the historic moment of prayer on March 27, 2020. It is meant not only to accompany the journey of the People of God in this historic moment, but also to help them see it as a moment of grace, the dawn of a *new creation*, for "even worse than this crisis is the tragedy of squandering it."

# *Urbi et Orbi* Message

Easter 2020

**Saint Peter's Basilica, Altar of Confession**
12 April 2020*

Dear brothers and sisters, Happy Easter!

Today the Church's proclamation echoes throughout the world: "Jesus Christ is risen!" – "He is truly risen!"

Like a new flame this Good News springs up in the night: the night of a world already faced with epochal challenges and now oppressed by a pandemic severely testing our whole human family. In this night, the Church's voice rings out: "Christ, my hope, has arisen!" (Easter Sequence).

This is a different "contagion," a message transmitted from heart to heart – for every human heart awaits this Good News. It is the contagion of hope: "Christ, my hope, is risen!" This is no magic formula that makes problems vanish. No, the resurrection of Christ is not that. Instead, it is the victory of love over the root of evil, a victory that does not "by-pass" suffering and death, but passes through them, opening a path in the abyss, transforming evil into good: this is the unique hallmark of the power of God.

The Risen Lord is also the Crucified One, not someone else. In his glorious body he bears indelible wounds: wounds that have become windows of hope. Let us turn our gaze to him that he may heal the wounds of an afflicted humanity.

Today my thoughts turn in the first place to the many who have been directly affected by the coronavirus: the sick, those who have died and family members who mourn the loss of their loved ones, to whom, in some cases, they were unable even to bid a final farewell. May the Lord of life welcome the departed into his kingdom and grant comfort and hope to those still suffering, especially the elderly and those who are alone. May he never withdraw his consolation and help from those who are especially vulnerable, such as persons who work in nursing homes, or live in barracks and prisons. For many, this is an Easter of solitude lived amid the sorrow and hardship that the pandemic is causing, from physical suffering to economic difficulties.

This disease has not only deprived us of human closeness, but also of the possibility of receiving in person the consolation that flows from the sacraments, particularly the Eucharist and

* http://www.vatican.va/content/francesco/en/messages/urbi/documents/papa-francesco_20200412_urbi-et-orbi-pasqua.html

Reconciliation. In many countries, it has not been possible to approach them, but the Lord has not left us alone! United in our prayer, we are convinced that he has laid his hand upon us (see *Ps* 138:5), firmly reassuring us: Do not be afraid, "I have risen and I am with you still!" (see *Roman Missal,* Entrance Antiphon, Mass of Easter Sunday).

May Jesus, our Passover, grant strength and hope to doctors and nurses, who everywhere offer a witness of care and love for our neighbors, to the point of exhaustion and not infrequently at the expense of their own health. Our gratitude and affection go to them, to all who work diligently to guarantee the essential services necessary for civil society, and to the law enforcement and military personnel who in many countries have helped ease people's difficulties and sufferings.

In these weeks, the lives of millions of people have suddenly changed. For many, remaining at home has been an opportunity to reflect, to withdraw from the frenetic pace of life, stay with loved ones and enjoy their company. For many, though, this is also a time of worry about an uncertain future, about jobs that are at risk and about other consequences of the current crisis. I encourage political leaders to work actively for the common good, to provide the means and resources needed to enable everyone to lead a dignified life and, when circumstances allow, to assist them in resuming their normal daily activities.

This is not a time for indifference, because the whole world is suffering and needs to be united in facing the pandemic. May the risen Jesus grant hope to all the poor, to those living on the peripheries, to refugees and the homeless. May these, the most vulnerable of our brothers and sisters living in the cities and peripheries of every part of the world, not be abandoned. Let us ensure that they do not lack basic necessities (all the more difficult to find now that many businesses are closed) such as medicine and especially the possibility of adequate health care. In light of the present circumstances, may international sanctions be relaxed, since these make it difficult for countries on which they have been imposed to provide adequate support to their citizens, and may all nations be put in a position to meet the greatest needs of the moment through the reduction, if not the forgiveness, of the debt burdening the balance sheets of the poorest nations.

This is not a time for self-centeredness, because the challenge we are facing is shared by all, without distinguishing between persons. Among the many areas of the world affected by the coronavirus, I think in a special way of Europe. After the Second World War, this continent was able to rise again, thanks to a concrete spirit of solidarity that enabled it to overcome the rivalries of the past. It is more urgent than ever, especially in the present circumstances, that these rivalries do not regain force, but that all recognize themselves as part of a single family and support one another. The European Union is presently facing an epochal challenge, on which will depend not only its future but that of the whole world. Let us not lose the opportunity to give further proof of solidarity, also by turning to innovative solutions. The only alternative is the selfishness of particular interests and the temptation of a return to the past, at the risk of severely damaging the peaceful coexistence and development of future generations.

This is not a time for division. May Christ our peace enlighten all who have responsibility in conflicts, that they may have the courage to support the appeal for an immediate global ceasefire in all corners of the world. This is not a time for continuing to manufacture and deal in arms, spending vast amounts of money that ought to be used to care for others and save lives. Rather, may this be a time for finally ending the long war that has caused such great bloodshed in beloved Syria, the conflict in Yemen and the hostilities in Iraq and in Lebanon. May this be the time when Israelis and Palestinians resume dialogue in order to find a stable and lasting solution that will allow both to live in peace. May the sufferings of the people who live in the eastern regions of Ukraine come to an end. May the terrorist attacks carried out against so many innocent people in different African countries come to an end.

This is not a time for forgetfulness. The crisis we are facing should not make us forget the many other crises that bring suffering to so many people. May the Lord of life be close to all those in Asia and Africa who are experiencing grave humanitarian crises, as in the Province of Cabo Delgado in the north of Mozambique. May he warm the hearts of the many refugees displaced because of wars, drought and famine. May he grant protection to migrants and refugees, many of them children, who are living in unbearable conditions, especially in Libya and on the border between Greece and Turkey. And I do not want to forget the island of Lesvos. In Venezuela, may he enable concrete and immediate solutions to be reached that can permit international assistance to a population suffering from the grave political, socioeconomic and health situation.

Dear brothers and sisters,

Indifference, self-centeredness, division and forgetfulness are not words we want to hear at this time. We want to ban these words forever! They seem to prevail when fear and death overwhelm us, that is, when we do not let the Lord Jesus triumph in our hearts and lives. May Christ, who has already defeated death and opened for us the way to eternal salvation, dispel the darkness of our suffering humanity and lead us into the light of his glorious day, a day that knows no end.

With these thoughts, I would like to wish all of you a happy Easter.

# A Plan to Rise up Again

**"*Vida Nueva*" Magazine**
17 April 2020*

"Suddenly Jesus met them and greeted them, saying: 'Rejoice'" (see *Mt* 28:9).

It is the first word of the Risen One after Mary Magdalene and the other Mary discovered the empty tomb and came across the angel. The Lord meets them to transform their mourning into joy and to comfort them in the midst of affliction (see *Jer* 31:13). He is the Risen One who wants to resurrect the women to a new life and, with them, all of humanity. He wants us to begin to participate from now in the resurrected condition that awaits us.

An invitation to joy could seem like a provocation, and even like a bad joke in the face of the serious consequences we are suffering from Covid-19. Like the disciples at Emmaus, some could think of it as a gesture of ignorance or irresponsibility (see *Lk* 24:17–19). Like the first disciples who went to the tomb, we have been living surrounded by an atmosphere of pain and uncertainty that makes us wonder: "Who will roll away the stone for us from the entrance to the tomb?" (*Mk* 16:3). How can we deal with this situation that has completely overwhelmed us? The impact of everything that is happening, the serious consequences that are already being reported, and those things which we have glimpsed, the pain and mourning for our loved ones, all have the capacity to disorient, distress and paralyze us. It is the heaviness of the tombstone that imposes itself on the future, and that threatens, with its realism, to bury all hope. It is the heaviness of the anguish of vulnerable people and elderly people who are going through quarantine in total solitude; it is the heaviness of those families who cannot now put a plate of food on their tables; it is the heaviness of health personnel and public servants feeling exhausted and overwhelmed ... that heaviness that seems to have the last word. However, it is moving to highlight the attitude of the women of the Gospel.

---

* The original text written in Spanish was published by« Vida Nueva » on 17 April 2020. This English translation has been carried out by LEV staff. https://www.vidanuevadigital.com/wp-content/uploads/2020/04/UN-PLAN-PARA-RESUCITAR-PAPA-FRANCISCO-VIDA-NUEVA.pdf

29 November 2015
**Opening of the Holy Door of the Cathedral of Bangui**

http://www.vatican.va/content/francesco/en/homilies/2015/documents/papa-francesco_20151129_repcentrafricana-omelia-cattedrale-bangui.html

Faced with doubts, suffering, perplexity in the face of the situation and even with fear of persecution and of everything that could happen to them, they were able to keep going and not be paralyzed by what was happening.

Out of love for the Master, and with that typical, irreplaceable and blessed feminine genius, they were able to confront life as it came, cunningly circumventing obstacles in order to be close to their Lord. Unlike many of the apostles who fled as prisoners of fear and insecurity – who denied the Lord and escaped (see *Jn* 18:25-27) – they [the women], without evading reality or ignoring what was happening, without fleeing or escaping ... they knew how to just be and to accompany others. The first women disciples, in the midst of darkness and grief, loaded their bags with perfumes and set out to anoint the buried Master (see *Mk* 16:1). Recently, we too, like them, have been able to see many who have sought to anoint others, through co-responsibility: they have offered care, and have avoided putting the lives of others at risk. Unlike those who fled with the hope of saving themselves, we witnessed how neighbors and family members set out with effort and sacrifice, to stay in their homes and thus curb the pandemic. We were able to discover how many people who were already living and suffering the pandemic of exclusion and indifference continued to strive, to accompany each other and to sustain themselves so that this situation is (or was) less painful. We saw anointing poured forth from doctors, nurses, supermarket shelf stackers, cleaners, carers, people who transport goods, agents of law and order, volunteers, priests, women religious, grandparents and educators and many others, who had the courage to offer everything they had, to bring some care, calm and courage to the situation. Although the question remained the same: "Who will roll away the stone from the tomb?" (*Mk* 16:3), all of them did not stop giving what they felt they could give, and had to give.

It was precisely there, in the midst of their cares and concerns, that the women disciples were surprised by an overwhelming announcement: "He is not here, he is risen." His anointing was not an anointing for death, but for life. Their watching and accompanying the Lord, even in death and in the midst of great despair, had not been in vain, but had allowed them to be anointed by the Resurrection: They were not alone, He was alive and preceded them on their way. Only this overwhelming piece of news was able to break the cycle which prevented them from seeing that the stone had already been rolled away; and that the perfume poured forth could diffuse further than the reality which threatened them.

This is the source of our joy and hope, which transforms our actions: Our anointings, dedication ... our watching and accompanying in all possible ways at this time are not, and will not be, in vain; they are not a dedication to death. Every time we take part in the Passion of the Lord, we accompany the passion of our brothers and sisters; living that same passion too, our ears will hear the novelty of the Resurrection: We are not alone, the Lord precedes us on our way, removing the stones that block us. This good news made those women retrace their steps to look for the apostles and the disciples who remained hidden, so as to tell them: He "reawakened to that same life (naturally in a new form) which death has destroyed."[1] This is our hope, the hope that cannot be stolen, silenced or contaminated. The whole life of service and love that you have given in this time will pulse again. It is enough to open a crack so that the anointing that the Lord wants to give us expands with an unstoppable force and allows us to contemplate the reality of suffering with a renewing outlook.

And, like the women of the Gospel, we too are invited again and again to retrace our steps and allow ourselves to be transformed by this announcement: the Lord, with his newness, can always renew our life and that of our community.[2] In this wasteland, the Lord is committed to the re-generation of beauty and the rebirth of hope: "Behold, I am doing something new: right now it is sprouting, don't you see it?" (*Is* 43:19). God never abandons his people, he is always close to them, especially when pain becomes more present.

If we have learned anything in all this time, it is that no one saves himself. Borders fall, walls collapse and all fundamentalist discourse dissolves before an almost imperceptible presence that manifests the fragility of which we are made. Easter summons us and invites us to remember His presence, which is discreet and respectful, generous and reconciling, capable of neither breaking the cracked reed nor extinguishing the wick that burns weakly (see *Is* 42:2–3); so that the new life that He wants to give us all, might pulsate. It is the breath of the Spirit that opens horizons, awakens creativity and renews us in fraternity to say I am *present* (or *here I am*) before the enormous and imperative task that awaits us. It is a matter of urgency to discern and find the pulse of the Spirit to give impetus, together with others, to dynamics that can witness and channel the new life that the Lord wants to generate at this concrete moment in history. This is the favorable time of the Lord, who is asking us not to conform or content ourselves, let alone justify ourselves with substitutive or palliative logic, which prevents us from sustaining the impact and serious consequences of what we are living. This is the right time to find the courage for a new imagination of the possible, with the realism that only the Gospel can offer us. The Spirit, who does not allow himself to be locked up or manipulated by fleeting or fixed schemes, modalities and structures, invites us to unite to his movement, which can "make all things new" (*Rv* 21:5).

In this time we realized that it is important "to bring the whole human family together to seek a sustainable and integral development."[3] Every individual action is not an isolated action, for better or for worse. It has consequences for others, because everything is interconnected in our common house; and if it is the health authorities who order confinement in the house, it is the people who make it possible, aware of their co-responsibility to curb the pandemic. "An emergency like that of Covid-19 is overcome with, above all, the antibodies of solidarity."[4] A lesson that will break all the fatalism in which we may have immersed ourselves, and this will allow us to feel once again as creators and protagonists of a common history and, thus, to respond together to so many evils that afflict millions of people around the world. We cannot afford to write present and future history by turning our backs on the suffering of so many. It is the Lord who will ask us again: "Where is your brother?" (*Gn* 4:9), and in the way we respond, may the soul of our peoples be revealed to us.

This is the reservoir of hope, faith and charity in which we have been born, and which, for so long, we have anesthetized and silenced. If we act as one people, even in the face of other epidemics that threaten us, we can make a real impact. Will we be able to act responsibly in the face of the hunger that so many suffer, knowing that there is food for all? Will we continue to look the other way with a complicit silence in the face of those wars fueled by desires for domination and power? Will we be willing to change those lifestyles that cause so many to suffer poverty, and promote and find the courage to lead a more austere and human life for a fair sharing of resources? Will we, as an international community, take the necessary measures to curb the devastation of the environment or will we continue to ignore the evidence? The globalization of indifference will continue to threaten and tempt us in our journey... May we find within us the necessary antibodies of justice, charity and solidarity. We must not be afraid to live the alternative – the civilization of love. This is "a civilization of hope: against anguish and fear, sadness and discouragement, passivity and tiredness. The civilization of love is built daily, uninterruptedly. It requires a committed effort by all. For this reason it requires a committed community of brothers and sisters."[5]

In this time of tribulation and mourning, I hope that, where you are, you will be able to experience Jesus, who comes to meet you, greets you and says: "Rejoice" (see *Mt* 28:9). And may this greeting mobilize us to invoke and amplify the Good News of the Kingdom of God.

[1] ROMANO GUARDINI, *The Lord,* Gateway Editions – Regnery Publications, Washington, DC 1996², 473.

[2] See Apostolic exhortation *Evangelii gaudium*, 24 November 2013, 11.

[3] Encyclical letter *Laudato si'*, 13.

[4] PONTIFICAL ACADEMY FOR LIFE, *Global Pandemic and Universal Brotherhood. Note on the Covid-19 Emergency*, 30 March 2020, 5.

[5] EDUARDO PIRONIO, *Diálogo con laicos*, Patria Grande, Buenos Aires 1986.

# Holy Mass | Second Sunday of Easter

## Homily

**Church of Santo Spirito in Sassia**
19 April 2020[*]

Last Sunday we celebrated the Lord's resurrection; today we witness the resurrection of his disciple. It has already been a week, a week since the disciples had seen the Risen Lord, but in spite of this, they remained fearful, cringing behind "closed doors" (*Jn* 20:26), unable even to convince Thomas, the only one absent, of the resurrection. What does Jesus do in the face of this timorous lack of belief? He returns and, standing in the same place, "in the midst" of the disciples, he repeats his greeting: "Peace be with you!" (*Jn* 20:19, 26). He starts all over. The resurrection of his disciple begins here, from this *faithful and patient mercy*, from the discovery that God never tires of reaching out to lift us up when we fall. He wants us to see him, not as a taskmaster with whom we have to settle accounts, but as our Father who always raises us up. In life we go forward tentatively, uncertainly, like a toddler who takes a few steps and falls; a few steps more and falls again, yet each time his father puts him back on his feet. The hand that always puts us back on our feet is mercy: God knows that without mercy we will remain on the ground, that in order to keep walking, we need to be put back on our feet.

You may object: "But I keep falling!" The Lord knows this and he is always ready to raise you up. He does not want us to keep thinking about our failings; rather, he wants us to look to him. For when we fall, he sees children needing to be put back on their feet; in our failings he sees children in need of his merciful love. Today, in this church that has become a shrine of mercy in Rome, and on this Sunday that Saint John Paul II dedicated to Divine Mercy twenty years ago, we confidently welcome this message. Jesus said to Saint Faustina: "I am love and mercy itself; there is no human misery that could measure up to my mercy" (*Diary*, 14 September 1937). At one time, the Saint, with satisfaction, told Jesus that she had offered him all of her life and all that she had. But Jesus' answer stunned her: "You have not offered me the thing is truly yours." What had that holy nun kept for herself? Jesus said to her with kindness: "My daughter, give me your failings" (10 October 1937). We too can ask ourselves: "Have I given my failings to the Lord? Have I let him see me fall so that he can raise me up?" Or is there something I still keep inside

[*] http://www.vatican.va/content/francesco/en/homilies/2020/documents/papa-francesco_20200419_omelia-divinamisericordia.html

me? A sin, a regret from the past, a wound that I have inside, a grudge against someone, an idea about a particular person. ... The Lord waits for us to offer him our failings so that he can help us experience his mercy.

Let us go back to the disciples. They had abandoned the Lord at his Passion and felt guilty. But meeting them, Jesus did not give a long sermon. To them, who were wounded within, he shows his own wounds. Thomas can now touch them and know of Jesus' love and how much Jesus had suffered for him, even though he had abandoned him. In those wounds, he touches with his hands God's tender closeness. Thomas arrived late, but once he received mercy, he overtook the other disciples: he believed not only in the resurrection, but in the boundless love of God. And he makes the most simple and beautiful profession of faith: "My Lord and my God!" (v. 28). Here is the resurrection of the disciple: it is accomplished when his frail and wounded humanity enters into that of Jesus. There, every doubt is resolved; there, God becomes *my God*; there, we begin to accept ourselves and to love life as it is.

Dear brothers and sisters, in the time of trial that we are presently undergoing, we too, like Thomas, with our fears and our doubts, have experienced our frailty. We need the Lord, who sees beyond that frailty an irrepressible beauty. With him we rediscover how precious we are even in our vulnerability. We discover that we are like beautiful crystals, fragile and at the same time precious. And if, like crystal, we are transparent before him, his light – the light of mercy – will shine in us and through us in the world. As the Letter of Peter said, this is a reason for being "filled with joy, though now for a little while you may have to suffer various trials" (*1 Pt* 1:6).

---

19 December 2019
**The life jacket and the cross remind us that we must keep our eyes open, keep our hearts open.**

https://www.vaticannews.va/en/pope/news/2019-12/pope-francis-it-s-injustice-that-causes-migrants-to-die-at-sea.html

"Once more we realized that no one is saved alone; we can only be saved together. As I said in those days, 'the storm has exposed our vulnerability and uncovered those false and superfluous certainties around which we constructed our daily schedules, our projects, our habits and priorities. ... Amid this storm, the façade of those stereotypes with which we camouflaged our egos, always worrying about appearances, has fallen away, revealing once more the ineluctable and blessed awareness that we are part of one another, that we are brothers and sisters of one another.'"

(Encyclical letter *Fratelli tutti*, 32)

On this feast of Divine Mercy, the most beautiful message comes from Thomas, the disciple who arrived late; he was the only one missing. But the Lord waited for Thomas. Mercy does not abandon those who stay behind. Now, while we are looking forward to a slow and arduous recovery from the pandemic, there is a danger that we will forget those who are left behind. The risk is that we may then be struck by an even worse virus, that of *selfish indifference*. A virus spread by the thought that life is better if it is better for me, and that everything will be fine if it is fine for me. It begins there and ends up selecting one person over another, discarding the poor, and sacrificing those left behind on the altar of progress. The present pandemic, however, reminds us that there are no differences or borders between those who suffer. We are all frail, all equal, all precious. May we be profoundly shaken by what is happening all around us: the time has come to eliminate inequalities, Healing the injustice that is undermining the health of the entire human family! Let us learn from the early Christian community described in the Acts of the Apostles. It received mercy and lived with mercy: "All who believed were together and had all things in common; and they sold their possessions and goods and distributed them to all, as any had need" (*Acts* 2:44–45). This is not some ideology: it is Christianity.

In that community, after the resurrection of Jesus, only one was left behind and the others waited for him. Today the opposite seems to be the case: a small part of the human family has moved ahead, while the majority has remained behind. Each of us could say: "These are complex problems, it is not my job to take care of the needy, others have to be concerned with it!" Saint Faustina, after meeting Jesus, wrote: "In a soul that is suffering we should see Jesus on the cross, not a parasite and a burden ... [Lord] you give us the chance to practice deeds of mercy, and we practice making judgments" (*Diary*, 6 September 1937). Yet she herself complained one day to Jesus that, in being merciful, one is thought to be naive. She said, "Lord, they often abuse my goodness." And Jesus replied: "Never mind, don't let it bother you, just be merciful to everyone always" (24 December 1937). To everyone: let us not think only of our interests, our vested interests. Let us welcome this time of trial as an opportunity to prepare for our collective future, a future for all without discarding anyone. Because without an all-embracing vision, there will be no future for anyone.

Today the simple and disarming love of Jesus revives the heart of his disciple. Like the apostle Thomas, let us accept mercy, the salvation of the world. And let us show mercy to those who are most vulnerable; for only in this way will we build a new world.

# Video Message on the Occasion
# Of the Pentecost Vigil Promoted by CHARIS

30 May 2020*

When the feast of Pentecost came, all the believers were gathered in one place. Thus begins the second chapter of the book of the Acts of the Apostles that we have just heard. Today too, thanks to technical advances, we are gathered together, believers from various parts of the world, on the eve of Pentecost.

The story continues: "Suddenly a sound like the blowing of a violent wind came from heaven and filled the whole house where they were sitting. They saw what seemed to be tongues of fire that separated and came to rest on each of them. All of them were filled with the Holy Spirit" (vv. 2–4).

The Spirit comes to rest on each of the disciples, on each one of us. The Spirit promised by Jesus comes to renew, to convert, to heal every one of us. He comes to cure us of our fears – how many fears we have! – our insecurities; He comes to heal our wounds, the wounds we also inflict on one another; and He comes to make us into disciples, missionary disciples, witnesses full of courage, of apostolic *parrhesia*, necessary for the preaching of the Gospel of Jesus, as we read in the following verses what happened to the disciples.

Today more than ever we need the Father to send us the Holy Spirit. In the first chapter of the Acts of the Apostles, Jesus says to His disciples: "Wait for the gift my Father promised, which you have heard me speak about. For John baptized with water, but in a few days you will be baptized with the Holy Spirit" (v. 4). And, in verse 8, He says to them: "You will receive power when the Holy Spirit comes on you; and you will be my witnesses in Jerusalem, and in all Judea and Samaria, and to the ends of the earth."

Witness of Jesus. The Holy Spirit leads us to this witness. Today the world suffers, it is wounded; we are living in a very wounded world, which suffers, especially the poorest, who are rejected, when all our human securities have disappeared, the world needs us to give it Jesus. We are able to give this witness only with the strength of the Holy Spirit.

---

* http://www.vatican.va/content/francesco/en/events/event.dir.html/content/vaticanevents/en/2020/5/30/videomessaggio-charis.html

We need the Spirit to give us new eyes, to open our mind and our heart so as to face this moment and the future with the lesson we have learned: we are a single humanity. We cannot save ourselves by ourselves. No one saves him or herself alone. No one. Saint Paul said, in the Letter to the Galatians: "There is neither Jew nor Gentile, neither slave nor free, nor is there male nor female, for you are all one in Christ Jesus" (3:28), united by the power of the Holy Spirit. Through this baptism of the Holy Spirit that Jesus announces. We know it, we knew it, but this pandemic we are living through has made us experience it in a much more dramatic way.

We have before us the duty to build a new reality. The Lord will do it; we can collaborate: "I make all things new," he says (*Rv* 21:5).

When we come out of this pandemic, we will no longer be able to do what we have been doing, how we have been doing it. No, everything will be different. All the suffering will have been pointless if we do not build together a more just, more equitable, more Christian society, not in name, but in reality, a reality that leads us to Christian behavior. If we do not work to end the pandemic of poverty in the world, the pandemic of poverty in the country of each one of us, in the city where each of us lives, this time will have been in vain.

From the great trials of humanity, including the pandemic, we emerge either better or worse. We do not come out the same.

I ask you: How do you want to come out of it? Better or worse? And that is why today we open ourselves up to the Holy Spirit so that he may change our hearts and help us to come out better.

If we do not live to be judged according to what Jesus tells us: "For I was hungry and you gave me food, I was thirsty and you gave me drink, a stranger and you welcomed me … in prison and you visited me" (*Mt* 25:35–36), then we will not come out of it better.

And this is a task for all of us, all of us. And also for you, members of charis, who are all the charismatics together.

The third document of Mechelen, written in the 1970s by Cardinal Suenens and Bishop Helder Camara, called: "Charismatic Renewal and Service of Man," marks this path in the current of grace. Be faithful to this call of the Holy Spirit!

I am reminded of the prophetic words of John XXIII when he announced the Vatican Council, and which Charismatic Renewal cherishes in particular: "May the Divine Spirit listen in the most comforting way to the prayer that ascends to Him from all corners of the earth: Renew in our time the wonders as of a new Pentecost, and grant that the Holy Church, remaining unanimous in prayer, with Mary, the Mother of Jesus and under the guidance of Peter, may increase the Kingdom of the Divine Savior, the Kingdom of Truth and Justice, the Kingdom of Love and Peace."

I wish for all of you, on this eve of Pentecost, the consolation of the Holy Spirit. And the strength of the Holy Spirit, to come out of this moment of pain, sadness and trial that is the pandemic; to come out of it better.

May the Lord bless you and the Virgin Mother keep you.

# Letter to the Priest of the Diocese of Rome

## Solennità di Pentecoste

31 May 2020*

Dear Brothers,

During this Easter season I had thought we could meet and celebrate the Chrism Mass together but, since a diocesan celebration was not possible, I am writing this letter to you. This new phase that we have embarked upon demands of us wisdom, farsightedness and shared commitment, so that all the efforts and sacrifices made thus far will not be in vain.

During this time of pandemic, many of you have shared with me by e-mail or telephone your experience of this unexpected and disconcerting situation. In this way, even though I was not able to leave home or encounter you directly, you let me know "first-hand" what you were going through. This in turn I have brought to my prayers, both of thanksgiving for your courageous and generous witness and of petition and trusting intercession before the Lord, who always takes us by the hand (see *Mt* 14:31). The need to maintain social distancing did not prevent us from strengthening our sense of fellowship, communion and mission; and this helped us ensure that charity, especially towards the most vulnerable individuals and communities, was not quarantined. In our frank conversations, I was able to see that necessary distancing was hardly synonymous with withdrawal or the self-absorption which anaesthetizes, sedates and extinguishes our sense of mission.

Encouraged by these exchanges, I am writing to you because I want to keep close to you and accompany, support and confirm you along the way. Hope also depends on our efforts, and we have to help one another to keep it alive and active. I mean that contagious hope which is cultivated and reaffirmed in the encounter with others, and which, as a gift and a task, is given to us in order to create the new "normality" that we so greatly desire.

In writing to you, I think of the early apostolic community, which also experienced moments of confinement, isolation, fear and uncertainty. Fifty days passed amid immobility, isolation, yet the first proclamation would change their lives forever. For even as the doors of the place where they stayed were closed out of fear, the disciples were surprised by Jesus who "stood among them and said, 'Peace be with you!' After he said this, he showed them his hands and side. The disciples were over-

* http://www.vatican.va/content/francesco/en/letters/2020/documents/papa-francesco_20200531_lettera-sacerdoti.html

joyed when they saw the Lord. Again Jesus said, 'Peace be with you! As the Father has sent me, I am sending you.' And with that he breathed on them and said, 'Receive the Holy Spirit'" (*Jn* 20:19–22). May we too let ourselves be surprised!

*The doors of the house where the disciples met were locked for fear* (*Jn* 20:19)

Today, as then, we sense that "the joys and the hopes, the griefs and the anxieties of the men of this age, especially those who are poor or in any way afflicted ... are the joys and hopes, the griefs and anxieties of the followers of Christ. Indeed, nothing genuinely human fails to raise an echo in their hearts" (*Gaudium et spes,* 1). How well we know this! We all listened to the numbers and percentages that daily bombarded us; with our own hands we touched the pain of our people. What we heard was not something alien to our own experience: the statistics had names, faces, stories of which we were a part. As a community of priests, we were no strangers to these situations; we did not look out at them from a window. Braving the tempest, you found ways to be present and accompany your communities; when you saw the wolf coming, you did not flee or abandon the flock (see *Jn* 10:12–13).

Suddenly we suffered the loss of family, neighbors, friends, parishioners, confessors, points of reference for our faith. We saw the saddened faces of those unable to be present and bid farewell to their loved ones in their final hours. We felt the suffering and powerlessness experienced by health care workers who, themselves exhausted, continued to work for days on end, out of a concern to meet so many needs. All of us felt the worry and fear experienced by those workers and volunteers who daily exposed themselves to risk in order to ensure that essential services were provided, and to accompany and care for the excluded and the vulnerable who were suffering even more from the effects of the pandemic. We witnessed the difficulties and discomforts of the lockdown: loneliness and isolation, especially among the elderly; anxiety, anguish and a sense of helplessness at the possibility of losing jobs and homes; violence and breakdown in relationships. The age-old fear of being infected once more reared its head. We shared the anguish and concern of entire families uncertain as to whether there would be food on the table in weeks to come.

We also experienced our own vulnerability and helplessness. Just as the kiln tests the potter's vases, so were we put to the test (see *Sir* 27:5). Distraught, we felt all the more the precariousness of our own lives and our apostolic efforts. The unpredictability of the situation heightened the difficulty we feel in facing the unknown which we cannot control or direct and, like everyone else, we felt confused, fearful and defenseless. At the same time, we also experienced that healthy and necessary courage that refuses to yield in the face of injustice and reminds us that we were created for Life. Like Nicodemus, at night, confused by the fact that "the wind blows where it wills, and you can hear the sound it makes, but you do not know where it comes from or where it goes," we too wondered: "How can this be?" And Jesus tells us too: "Are you are a teacher of Israel, yet you do not understand these things?" (see *Jn* 3:8–10).

The complexity of the situation we had to face did not allow for textbook recipes or responses. It called for something much more than facile exhortations or edifying speeches incapable of touching hearts and confronting the concrete demands of life. The pain of our people was our pain, their uncertainties our own: our shared sense of frailty stripped us of any pseudo-spiritual complacency or any puritanical attempt to keep at a safe distance. No one can be unaffected by all that has happened. We can say that *we experienced as a community the time when the Lord wept*: for we too wept before the tomb of Lazarus his friend (see *Jn* 11:35), before the incomprehension of his people (*Lk* 13:14; 19:41), in the dark night of Gethsemane (see *Mk* 14:32–42; *Lk* 22:44). *It is also the time when his disciples weep* before the mystery of the cross and the evil which strikes so many innocent people. It is the bitter weeping of Peter after his denial (see *Lk* 22:62), and that of Mary Magdalene before the tomb (see *Jn* 20:11).

We know that, in situations like these, it is not easy to find the right way forward, and any number of voices will make themselves heard telling us about all that could have been done in the face of this unknown reality. Our usual ways of relating, planning, celebrating, praying, meeting and even dealing with conflict were changed and challenged by an invisible presence that turned our everyday existence upside down. Nor did it simply affect individuals, families, specific social groups or countries. The nature of the virus caused our former ways of dividing and classifying reality to disappear. The pandemic knows no descriptors, no boundaries, and none of us can think of getting by alone. We are all affected and involved.

The notion of a "safe" society, carefree and poised for infinite consumption has been called into question, revealing its lack of cultural and spiritual immunity to conflict. A series of old and new questions and problems (in many places long since considered resolved) came to dominate the horizon and our attention. Those questions will not be answered simply by resuming various activities. They necessarily challenge us to develop a capacity for listening in a way attentive yet filled with hope, serene yet tenacious, persevering yet not fearful. This can prepare and open up the path that the Lord is now calling us to take (see *Mk* 1:2–3). We know that in the wake of tribulation and painful experiences we are never again the same. So all of us need to be vigilant and attentive. The Lord himself, in the hour of his own suffering, prayed for exactly this: "I do not ask that you take them out of the world, but that you keep them from the evil one" (*Jn* 17:15). Having experienced, as individuals and in our communities, our vulnerability, frailty and limitations, we now run the grave risk of withdrawing and "brooding" over the desolation caused by the pandemic, or else that of seeking refuge in a boundless optimism incapable of grasping the deeper meaning of what is happening all around us.[1]

Times of tribulation challenge us to discern the temptations that threaten to mire us in bewilderment and confusion, in a mind-set that would prevent our communities from nurturing the new life that the Risen Lord wishes to give us. A variety of temptations can nowadays blind us and encourage sentiments and approaches that block hope from stimulating our creativity, our ingenuity and our ability to respond effectively. Rather than seeking to acknowledge frankly the gravity of the situation, we can attempt to respond merely with new and reassuring activities as we wait for everything to "return to normal." But in this way we would ignore the deep wounds that have opened and the number of people who have fallen in the meantime. We can also sink into in a kind of numbing nostalgia for the recent past that leads us to keep repeating that "nothing will ever be the same again" and thus show ourselves incapable of inviting others to dream and to develop new paths and new styles of life.

*Jesus came and stood in their midst and said to them, "Peace be with you." When he had said this, he showed them his hands and his side. The disciples rejoiced when they saw the Lord. Jesus said to them again, "Peace be with you!" (Jn 20:19–21)*

The Lord did not choose the perfect situation to appear suddenly in the midst of his disciples. Certainly we would have preferred that what happened did not have to happen, but it did; and like the disciples on the road to Emmaus, we too can continue to speak sadly and in hushed tones along the way (see *Lk* 24:13–21). Yet by appearing in the Upper Room behind closed doors, amid the isolation, fear and insecurity experienced by the disciples, the Lord was able to surpass all expectations and to give a new meaning to history and human events. Any time is fitting for the message of peace; in no situation is God's grace ever lacking. Jesus' appearance in the midst of confinement and forced absence proclaims, for those disciples and for us today, a new day capable of challenging all paralysis and resignation, and harnessing every gift for the service of the community. By his presence, confinement became fruitful, giving life to the new apostolic community.

So let us say with confidence and without fear: "Where sin increased, grace has abounded all the more" (*Rom* 5:20). Let us be fearless amid the messy situations all around us, because that is where the Lord is, in our midst; God continues to perform his miracle of bringing forth good fruit (see *Jn* 15:5). Christian joy is born precisely of this certainty. In the midst of the contradictions and perplexities we must confront each day, the din of so many words and opinions, there is the quiet voice of the Risen Lord who keeps saying to us: "Peace be with you!"

It is comforting to read the Gospel and think of Jesus in the midst of his people, as he welcomes and embraces life and individuals just as they are. His actions embody Mary's moving song of praise: "He has shown strength with his arm; he has scattered the proud in the thoughts of their hearts. He has brought down the powerful from their thrones, and lifted up the lowly" (*Lk* 1:51–52). Jesus offers his own hands and his wounded side as a path to resurrection. He does not hide or conceal those wounds; instead, he invites Thomas to touch his pierced side and to see how those very wounds can be the source of Life in abundance (see *Jn* 20:27–29).

Over and over again, as a spiritual guide, I have been able to witness how "a person who sees things as they truly are and sympathizes with pain and sorrow is capable of touching life's depths and finding authentic happiness. He or she is consoled, not by the world but by Jesus. Such persons are unafraid to share in the suffering of others; they do not flee from painful situations. They discover the meaning of life by coming to the aid of those who suffer, understanding their anguish and bringing relief. They sense that the other is flesh of our flesh, and are not afraid to draw near, even to touch their wounds. They feel compassion for others in such a way that all distance vanishes. In this way, they can embrace Saint Paul's exhortation: 'Weep with those who weep' (*Rom* 12:15). Knowing how to mourn with others: that is holiness."[2]

*"As the Father has sent me, so I send you" When he had said this, he breathed on them and said to them: "Receive the Holy Spirit"* (*Jn* 20:21–22)

Dear brothers, as a community of priests, we are called to proclaim and prophesy the future, like the sentinel announcing the dawn that brings a new day (see *Is* 21:11). That new day will either be completely new, or something much worse than what we have been used to. The Resurrection is not simply an event of past history to be remembered and celebrated; it is much more. It is the saving proclamation of a new age that resounds and already bursts onto the scene: "Now it springs up; do you not perceive it?" (*Is* 43:19); it is the future, the "ad-vent" that the Lord even now is calling us to build. Faith grants us a realistic and creative imagination, one capable of abandoning the mentality of repetition, substitution and maintenance. An imagination that calls us to bring about a time ever new: the time of the Lord. Though an invisible, silent, expansive and viral presence has thrown us into crisis and turmoil, may we let this other discreet, respectful and non-invasive Presence summon us anew and teach us to face reality without fear. If an impalpable presence has been able to disrupt and upset the priorities and apparently overpowering global agendas that suffocate and devastate our communities and our sister earth, let us not be afraid to let the presence of the Risen Lord point out our path, open new horizons and grant us the courage to live to the full this unique moment of our history. A handful of fearful men were able to change the course of history by courageously proclaiming the God who is with us. Do not be afraid! "The powerful witness of the saints is revealed in their lives, shaped by the Beatitudes and the criterion of the final judgment."[3]

Let us be surprised yet again by the Risen Lord. May he, whose pierced side is a sign of how harsh and unjust reality can be, encourage us not to turn aside from the harsh and difficult realities experienced by our brothers and sisters. May he teach us how to accompany, soothe and bind up the wounds of our people, not with fear but with the audacity and evangelical generosity of the multiplication of the loaves (*Mt* 14:15–21); with the courage, concern and responsibility of the Good Samaritan (see *Lk* 10:33–35); with the joy of the shepherd at his newfound sheep (*Lk* 15:4–6); with the reconciling embrace of a father who knows the meaning of forgiveness (see *Lk* 15:20); with the devotion, gentleness and tender love of Mary of Bethany (see *Jn* 12:1–3); with the meekness, patience and wisdom of the Lord's missionary disciples (see *Mt* 10:16–23). May the wounded hands of the Risen Lord console us in our sorrows, revive our hope and impel us to seek the Kingdom of God by stepping out of our familiar surroundings . Let us also allow ourselves to be surprised by our good and faithful people, so often tried and torn, yet also visited by the Lord's mercy. May our people teach us, their pastors, how to mold and temper our hearts with meekness and compassion, with the humility and magnanimity of a lively, supportive, patient and courageous perseverance, one that does not remain indifferent, but rejects and unmasks every form of scepticism and fatalism. How much we have to learn from the strength of God's faithful people, who always find a way to help and accompany those who have fallen! The Resurrection is the proclamation that things can change. May the Paschal Mystery, which knows no bounds, lead us creatively to those places where hope and life are struggling, where suffering and pain are opening the door to corruption and speculation, where aggression and violence appear to be the only way out.

As priests, sons and members of a priestly people, it is up to us to take responsibility for the future and to plan for it as brothers. Let us place in the wounded hands of the Lord, as a holy offering, our own weakness, the weakness of our people and that of all humanity. It is the Lord who transforms us, who treats us like bread, taking our life into his hands, blessing us, breaking and sharing us, and giving us to his people. And in all humility, let us allow ourselves to be anointed by Paul's words and let them spread like a fragrant balm throughout our City, thus awakening the seeds of hope that so many people quietly nurture in their hearts: "We are afflicted in every way, but not crushed; perplexed, but not driven to despair; persecuted, but not abandoned; struck down, but not destroyed; always carrying in the body the dying of Jesus, so that the life of Jesus may also be made visible in our bodies" (*2 Cor* 4:8–10). Let us share with Jesus in his passion, our passion, and experience, also with him, the power of the Resurrection: the certainty of God's love that affects us deeply and summons us to take to the streets in order to bring "glad tidings to the poor … to proclaim liberty to captives and recovery of sight to the blind, to let the oppressed go free, and to proclaim a year acceptable to the Lord" (see *Lk* 4:18–19), with a joy that all can share in their dignity as children of the living God.

All these things, which I have been thinking about and experiencing during this time of pandemic, I want to share fraternally with you, so that they can help us on our journey of praising the Lord and serving our brothers and sisters. I hope that they can prove useful to each of us, for "ever greater love and service."

May the Lord Jesus bless you and the Blessed Virgin watch over you. And please, do not forget to keep me in your prayers.

Fraternally,

**Francesco**

---

¹ See *Evangelii gaudium*, 226–228.
² *Gaudete et exsultate*, 76.
³ *Ibid.*, 109.

# Video Message on the occasion of the 75<sup>th</sup> Meeting of the General Assembly of the United Nations

25 September 2020*

Mr. President,

Peace be with all of you!

I offer cordial greetings to you, Mr. President, and to all the Delegations taking part in this significant Seventy-fifth Session of the United Nations' General Assembly. In particular, I greet the Secretary General, Mr. António Guterres, the participating Heads of State and Government, and all those who are following the General Debate.

The seventy-fifth anniversary of the United Nations offers me a fitting occasion to express once again the Holy See's desire that this Organization increasingly serve as a sign of unity between States and an instrument of service to the entire human family.[1]

In these days, our world continues to be impacted by the Covid-19 pandemic, which has led to the loss of so many lives. This crisis is changing our way of life, calling into question our economic, health and social systems, and exposing our human fragility.

The pandemic, indeed, calls us "to seize this time of trial as a time of choosing, a time to choose what matters and what passes away, a time to separate what is necessary from what is not."[2] It can represent a concrete opportunity for conversion, for transformation, for rethinking our way of life and our economic and social systems, which are widening the gap between rich and poor based on an unjust distribution of resources. On the other hand, the pandemic can be the occasion for a "defensive retreat" into greater individualism and elitism.

We are faced, then, with a choice between two possible paths. One path leads to the consolidation of multilateralism as the expression of a renewed sense of global co-responsibility, a solidarity grounded in justice and the attainment of peace and unity within the human family, which is God's plan for our world. The other path emphasizes self-sufficiency, nationalism, protectionism, individualism and isolation; it excludes the poor, the vulnerable and those dwelling on the peripheries of life. That path would certainly be detrimental to the whole community, causing self-inflicted wounds on everyone. It must not prevail.

* http://www.vatican.va/content/francesco/en/messages/pont-messages/2020/documents/papa-francesco_20200925_videomessaggio-onu.html

The pandemic has highlighted the urgent need to promote public health and to make every person's right to basic medical care a reality.[3] For this reason, I renew my appeal to political leaders and the private sector to spare no effort to ensure access to Covid-19 vaccines and to the essential technologies needed to care for the sick. If anyone should be given preference, let it be the poorest, the most vulnerable, those who so often experience discrimination because they have neither power nor economic resources.

The current crisis has also demonstrated that solidarity must not be an empty word or promise. It has also shown us the importance of avoiding every temptation to exceed our natural limits. "We *have* the freedom needed to limit and direct technology; we *can* put it at the service of another type of progress, one which is healthier, more human, more social, more integral."[4] This also needs to be taken into careful consideration in discussions on the complex issue of artificial intelligence (AI).

Along these same lines, I think of the effects of the pandemic on employment, a sector already destabilized by a labor market driven by increasing uncertainty and widespread robotization. There is an urgent need to find new forms of work truly capable of fulfilling our human potential and affirming our dignity. In order to ensure dignified employment, there must be a change in the prevailing economic paradigm, which seeks only to expand companies' profits. Offering jobs to more people should be one of the main objectives of every business, one of the criteria for the success of productive activity. Technological progress is valuable and necessary, provided that it serves to make people's work more dignified and safe, less burdensome and stressful.

All this calls for a change of direction. To achieve this, we already possess the necessary cultural and technological resources, and social awareness. This change of direction will require, however, a more robust ethical framework capable of overcoming "today's widespread and quietly growing culture of waste."[5]

At the origin of this "throwaway culture" is a gross lack of respect for human dignity, the promotion of ideologies with reductive understandings of the human person, a denial of the universality of fundamental human rights, and a craving for absolute power and control that is widespread in today's society. Let us name this for what it is: an attack against humanity itself.

It is in fact painful to see the number of fundamental human rights that in our day continue to be violated with impunity. The list of such violations is indeed lengthy, and offers us a frightening picture of a humanity abused, wounded, deprived of dignity, freedom and hope for the future. As part of this picture, religious believers continue to endure every kind of persecution, including genocide, because of their beliefs. We Christians too are victims of this: how many of our brothers and sisters throughout the world are suffering, forced at times to flee from their ancestral lands, cut off from their rich history and culture.

We should also admit that humanitarian crises have become the *status quo*, in which people's right to life, liberty and personal security are not protected. Indeed, as shown by conflicts worldwide, the use of explosive weapons, especially in populated areas, is having a dramatic long-term humanitarian impact. Conventional weapons are becoming less and less "conventional" and more and more "weapons of mass destruction," wreaking havoc on cities, schools, hospitals, religious sites, infrastructures and basic services needed by the population.

What is more, great numbers of people are being forced to leave their homes. Refugees, migrants and the internally displaced frequently find themselves abandoned in their countries of origin, transit and destination, deprived of any chance to better their situation in life and that of their families. Worse still, thousands are intercepted at sea and forcibly returned to detention camps, where they meet with torture and abuse. Many of these become victims of human trafficking, sexual slavery or forced labor, exploited in degrading jobs and denied a just wage. This is intolerable, yet intentionally ignored by many!

The numerous and significant international efforts to respond to these crises begin with great promise – here I think of the two Global Compacts on Refugees and on Migration – yet many lack the necessary political support to prove successful. Others fail because individual states shirk their responsibilities and commitments. All the same, the current crisis offers an opportunity for the United Nations to help build a more fraternal and compassionate society.

This includes reconsidering the role of economic and financial institutions, like that of Bretton-Woods, which must respond to the rapidly growing inequality between the super-rich and the permanently poor. An economic model that encourages subsidiarity, supports economic development at the local level and invests in education and infrastructure benefiting local communities, will lay the foundation not only for economic success but also for the renewal of the larger community and nation. Here I would renew my appeal that "in light of the present circumstances … all nations be enabled to meet the greatest needs of the moment through the reduction, if not the forgiveness, of the debt burdening the balance sheets of the poorest nations."[6]

The international community ought to make every effort to put an end to economic injustices. "When multilateral credit organizations provide advice to various nations, it is important to keep in mind the lofty concepts of fiscal justice, the public budgets responsible for their indebtedness and, above all, an effective promotion of the poorest, which makes them protagonists in the social network."[7] We have a responsibility to offer development assistance to poor nations and debt relief to highly indebted nations.[8]

"A new ethics presupposes being aware of the need for everyone to work together to close tax shelters, avoid evasions and money laundering that rob society, as well as to speak to nations about the importance of defending justice and the common good over the interests of the most powerful companies and multinationals."[9] Now is a fitting time to renew the architecture of international finance.[10]

Mr. President,

Five years ago, I had the opportunity to address the General Assembly in person on its seventieth anniversary. My visit took place at a time marked by truly dynamic multilateralism. It was a moment of great hope and promise for the international community, on the eve of the adoption of the 2030 Agenda for Sustainable Development. Some months later, the Paris Agreement on Climate Change was also adopted.

Yet we must honestly admit that, even though some progress has been made, the international community has shown itself largely incapable of honoring the promises made five years ago. I can only reiterate that "we must avoid every temptation to fall into a declarationist nominalism which would assuage our consciences. We need to ensure that our institutions are truly effective in the struggle against all these scourges."[11]

I think of the alarming situation in the Amazon and its indigenous peoples. Here we see that the environmental crisis is inseparably linked to a social crisis, and that caring for the environment calls for an integrated approach to combatting poverty and exclusion.[12]

To be sure, the growth of an integral ecological sensitivity and the desire for action is a positive step. "We must not place the burden on the next generations to take on the problems caused by the previous ones. … We must seriously ask ourselves if there is the political will to allocate with honesty, responsibility and courage, more human, financial and technological resources to mitigate the negative effects of climate change, as well as to help the poorest and most vulnerable populations who suffer from them the most."[13]

The Holy See will continue to play its part. As a concrete sign of the Holy See's commitment to care for our common home, I recently ratified the Kigali Amendment to the Montreal Protocol.[14]


Mr. President,

We cannot fail to acknowledge the devastating effects of the Covid-19 crisis on children, including unaccompanied young migrants and refugees. Violence against children, including the horrible scourge of child abuse and pornography, has also dramatically increased.

Millions of children are presently unable to return to school. In many parts of the world, this situation risks leading to an increase in child labor, exploitation, abuse and malnutrition. Sad to say, some countries and international institutions are also promoting abortion as one of the so-called "essential services" provided in the humanitarian response to the pandemic. It is troubling to see how simple and convenient it has become for some to deny the existence of a human life as a solution to problems that can and must be solved for both the mother and her unborn child.

I urge civil authorities to be especially attentive to children who are denied their fundamental rights and dignity, particularly their right to life and to schooling. I cannot help but think of the appeal of that courageous young woman, Malala Yousafzai, who speaking five years ago in the General Assembly, reminded us that "one child, one teacher, one book and one pen can change the world."

The first teachers of every child are his or her mother and father, the family, which the Universal Declaration of Human Rights describes as the "natural and fundamental group unit of society."[15] All too often, the family is the victim of forms of ideological colonialism that weaken it and end up producing in many of its members, especially the most vulnerable, the young and the elderly, a feeling of being orphaned and lacking roots. The breakdown of the family is reflected in the social fragmentation that hinders our efforts to confront common enemies. It is time that we reassess and recommit ourselves to achieving our goals.

One such goal is the advancement of women. This year marks the twenty-fifth anniversary of the Beijing Conference on Women. At every level of society, women now play an important role, offering their singular contribution and courageously promoting the common good. Many women, however, continue to be left behind: victims of slavery, trafficking, violence, exploitation and degrading treatment. To them, and to those who forced to live apart from their families, I express my fraternal closeness. At the same time, I appeal once more for greater determination and commitment in the fight against those heinous practices that debase not only women, but all humanity, which by its silence and lack of effective action becomes an accomplice in them.


Mr. President,

We must ask ourselves if the principal threats to peace and security – poverty, epidemics, terrorism and so many others – can  effectively be countered when the arms race, including nuclear weapons, continues to squander precious resources that could better be used to benefit the integral development of peoples and protect the natural environment.

We need to break with the present climate of distrust. At present, we are witnessing an erosion of multilateralism, which is all the more serious in light of the development of new forms of military technology,[16] such as lethal autonomous weapons systems (LAWS) which irreversibly alter the nature of warfare, detaching it further from human agency.

We need to dismantle the perverse logic that links personal and national security to the possession of weaponry. This logic serves only to increase the profits of the arms industry, while fostering a climate of distrust and fear between persons and peoples.

Nuclear deterrence, in particular, creates an ethos of fear based on the threat of mutual annihilation; in this way, it ends up poisoning relationships between peoples and obstructing dialogue.[17] That is why it is so important to support the principal international legal instruments on nuclear disarmament, non-proliferation and prohibition. The Holy See trusts that the forthcoming Review Conference of the Parties to the Treaty on the Non-Proliferation of Nuclear Weapons (NPT) will result in concrete action in accordance with our joint intention "to achieve at the earliest possible date the cessation of the nuclear arms race and to undertake effective measures in the direction of nuclear disarmament."[18]

In addition, our strife-ridden world needs the United Nations to become an ever more effective international workshop for peace. This means that the members of the Security Council, especially the Permanent Members, must act with greater unity and determination. In this regard, the recent adoption of a global cease-fire during the present crisis is a very noble step, one that demands good will on the part of all for its continued implementation. Here I would also reiterate the importance of relaxing international sanctions that make it difficult for states to provide adequate support for their citizens.


Mr. President,

We never emerge from a crisis just as we were. We come out either better or worse. This is why, at this critical juncture, it is our duty *to rethink the future of our common home and our common project*. A complex task lies before us, one that requires a frank and coherent dialogue aimed at strengthening multilateralism and cooperation between states. The present crisis has further demonstrated the limits of our self-sufficiency as well as our common vulnerability. It has forced us to think clearly about how we want to emerge from this: either better or worse.

The pandemic has shown us that we cannot live without one another, or worse still, pitted against one another. The United Nations was established to bring nations together, to be a bridge between peoples. Let us make good use of this institution in order to transform the challenge that lies before us into an opportunity to build together, once more, the future we all desire.

God bless you all!


Thank you, Mr. President.

[1] *Address to the General Assembly of the United Nations*, 25 September 2015; Benedict XVI, *Address to the General Assembly of the United Nations*, 18 April 2008.

[2] *Extraordinary Moment of Prayer in the Time of Epidemic*, 27 March 2020.

[3] *Universal Declaration of Human Rights*, Article 25.1.

[4] *Laudato Si'*, 112.

[5] *Address to the General Assembly of the United Nations Organization*, 25 September 2015.

[6] *Urbi et Orbi Message*, 12 April 2020.

[7] *Address to the Participants in the Seminar "New Forms of Solidarity,"* 5 February 2020.

[8] See *ibid.*

[9] *Ibid.*

[10] See *ibid.*

[11] *Address to the General Assembly of the United Nations Organization*, 25 September 2015.

[12] *Laudato Si'*, 139.

[13] *Message to the Participants in the Twenty-Fifth Session of the Conference of States Parties to the United Nations Framework Convention on Climate Change*, 1 December 2019.

[14] *Message to the Thirty-first Meeting of the Parties to the Montreal Protocol*, 7 November 2019.

[15] *Universal Declaration of Human Rights*, Article 16.3.

[16] *Address on Nuclear Weapons*, Atomic Bomb Hypocenter Park, Nagasaki, 24 November 2019.

[17] *Ibid.*

[18] *Treaty on the Non-Proliferation of Nuclear Weapons*, Preamble.

# Wednesday Audience Catechesis | Healing the world

## General Audiences | 5 August – 30 September 2020

## 1. Introduction

**Library of the Apostolic Palace**
5 August 2020*

Dear brothers and sisters, good morning!

The pandemic continues to cause deep wounds, exposing our vulnerability. On every continent there are many who have died, many are ill. Many people and many families are living a time of uncertainty because of socioeconomic problems which especially affect the poorest.

Thus, we must keep our gaze firmly fixed on Jesus (see *Heb* 12:2): in the midst of this pandemic, our eyes on Jesus; and with this *faith* embrace the *hope* of the Kingdom of God that Jesus Himself brings us (see *Mk* 1:5; *Mt* 4:17; *Catechism of the Catholic Church*, 2816). A Kingdom of healing and of salvation that is already present in our midst (see *Lk* 10:11). A Kingdom of justice and of peace that is manifested through works of *charity*, which in their turn increase hope and strengthen faith (see *1 Cor* 13:13). Within the Christian tradition, *faith, hope and charity* are much more than feelings or attitudes. They are virtues infused in us through the grace of the Holy Spirit:[1] gifts that heal us and that make us healers, gifts that open us to new horizons, even while we are navigating the difficult waters of our time.

Renewed contact with the Gospel of faith, of hope and of love invites us to assume a creative and renewed spirit. In this way, we will be able to transform the roots of our physical, spiritual and social infirmities and the destructive practices that separate us from each other, threatening the human family and our planet.

Jesus' ministry offers many examples of healing: when He heals those affected by fever (see *Mk* 1:29–34), by leprosy (see *Mk* 1:40–45), by paralysis (see *Mk* 2:1–12); when He restores sight (see *Mk* 8:22–26; *Jn* 9:1–7), speech or hearing (see *Mk* 7:31–37). In reality, He heals not only the physical evil – which is true, physical evil – but He heals the entire person. In that way, He restores the person back to the community also, healed; He liberates the person from isolation because He has healed him or her.

Let's think of the beautiful account of the healing of the paralytic at Capernaum (see *Mk* 2:1–12) that we heard at the beginning of the audience. While Jesus is preaching at the entrance to the house, four men bring their paralyzed friend to Jesus. Not being able to enter because there was

* http://www.vatican.va/content/francesco/en/audiences/2020/documents/papa-francesco_20200805_udienza-generale.html

such a great crowd there, they make a hole in the roof and let the stretcher down in front of Him. Jesus who was preaching sees this stretcher coming down in front of Him. "When Jesus saw their faith, he said to the paralytic, 'Child, your sins are forgiven'" (v. 5). And then, as a visible sign, He adds: "Rise, pick up your mat, and go home" (v. 11).

What a wonderful example of healing! Christ's action is a direct response to the faith of those people, to the hope they put in Him, to the love they show that they have for each other. And so, Jesus heals, but He does not simply heal the paralysis. Jesus heals everyone, He forgives sins, He renews the life of the paralyzed man and his friend. He makes him born again, let's say it that way. It is a physical and spiritual healing, all together, the fruit of personal and social contact. Let's imagine how this friendship, and the faith of all those present in that house, would have grown thanks to Jesus' action, that healing encounter with Jesus!

And so we can ask ourselves: today, in what way can we help heal our world? As disciples of the Lord Jesus, who is the physician of our souls and bodies, we are called to continue "His work, work of healing and salvation"[2] in a physical, social and spiritual sense.

Although the Church administers Christ's healing grace through the Sacraments, and although she provides healthcare services in the remotest corners of the planet, she is not an expert in the prevention or the cure of the pandemic. She helps with the sick, but she is not an expert. Neither does she give specific sociopolitical pointers.[3] This is the job of political and social leaders. Nevertheless, over the centuries, and by the light of the Gospel, the Church has developed several social principles which are fundamental,[4] principles that can help us move forward in preparing the future that we need. I cite the main ones which are closely connected: the principle of the dignity of the person, the principle of the common good, the principle of the preferential option for the poor, the principle of the universal destination of goods, the principle of the solidarity, of subsidiarity, the principle of the care for our common home. These principles help the leaders, those responsible for society, to foster growth and also, as in the case of the pandemic, the healing of the personal and social fabric. All of these principles express in different ways the virtues of faith, hope and love.

In the next few weeks, I invite you to tackle together the pressing questions that the pandemic has brought to the fore, social ills above all. And we will do it in the light of the Gospel, of the theological virtues and of the principles of the Church's social doctrine. We will explore together how our Catholic social tradition can help the human family heal this world that suffers from serious illnesses. It is my desire that everyone reflect and work together, as followers of Jesus who heals, to construct a better world, full of hope for future generations.[5] Thank you.

---

[1] See *Catechism of the Catholic Church*, 1812; 1813.
[2] *Catechism of the Catholic Church*, 1421.
[3] See St. Paul VI, Apostolic letter *Octogesima adveniens*, 4.
[4] See *Compendium of the Social Doctrine of the Church*, 160–208.
[5] See *Evangelii gaudium*, 183.

## 2. Faith and human dignity

**Library of the Apostolic Palace**
12 August 2020*

Dear brothers and sisters, good morning!

The pandemic has highlighted how vulnerable and interconnected everyone is. If we do not take care of one another, starting with the least, with those who are most impacted, including creation, we cannot heal the world.

Commendable is the effort of so many people who have been offering evidence of human and Christian love for neighbor, dedicating themselves to the sick even at the risk of their own health. They are heroes! However, the coronavirus is not the only disease to be fought, but rather, the pandemic has shed light on broader social ills. One of these is a distorted view of the person, a perspective that ignores the dignity and relational nature of the person. At times we look at others as objects, to be used and discarded. In reality this type of perspective blinds and fosters an individualistic and aggressive throw-away culture, which transforms the human being into a consumer good.[1]

In the light of faith we know, instead, that God looks at a man and a woman in another manner. He created us not as objects but as people loved and capable of loving; He has created us in His image and likeness (see *Gn* 1:27). In this way He has given us a unique dignity, calling us to live in communion with Him, in communion with our sisters and our brothers, with respect for all creation. In communion, in harmony, we might say. Creation is the harmony in which we are called to live. And in this communion, in this harmony that is communion, God gives us the ability to procreate and safeguard life (see *Gn* 1:28–29), to till and keep the land (see *Gn* 2:15; *Laudato si'*, 67). It is clear that one cannot procreate and safeguard life without harmony; it will be destroyed.

We have an example of that individualistic perspective, that which is not harmony, in the Gospels, in the request made to Jesus by the mother of the disciples James and John (see *Mt* 20:20–38). She wanted her sons to sit at the right and the left of the new king. But Jesus proposes another type of vision: that of service and of giving one's life for others, and He confirms it by immediately restoring sight to two blind men and making them His disciples (see *Mt* 20:29–34). Seeking to climb in life, to be superior to others, destroys harmony. It is the logic of dominion, of dominating others. Harmony is something else: it is service.

* http://www.vatican.va/content/francesco/en/audiences/2020/documents/papa-francesco_20200812_udienza-generale.html

Therefore, let us ask the Lord to give us eyes attentive to our brothers and sisters, especially those who are suffering. As Jesus' disciples we do not want to be indifferent or individualistic. These are the two unpleasant attitudes that run counter to harmony. Indifferent: I look the other way. Individualist: looking out only for one's own interest. The harmony created by God asks that we look at others, the needs of others, the problems of others, in communion. We want to recognize the human dignity in every person, whatever his or her race, language or condition might be. Harmony leads you to recognize human dignity, that harmony created by God, with humanity at the center.

The Second Vatican Council emphasizes that this dignity is inalienable, because it "was created 'to the image of God.'"[2] It lies at the foundation of all social life and determines its operative principles. In modern culture, the closest reference to the principle of the inalienable dignity of the person is the Universal Declaration of Human Rights, which Saint John Paul II defined as a "milestone on the long and difficult path of the human race,"[3] and as "one of the highest expressions of the human conscience."[4] Rights are not only individual, but also social; they are of peoples, nations.[5] The human being, indeed, in his or her personal dignity, is a social being, created in the image of God, One and Triune. We are social beings; we need to live in this social harmony, but when there is selfishness, our outlook does not reach others, the community, but focuses on ourselves, and this makes us ugly, nasty and selfish, destroying harmony.

This renewed awareness of the dignity of every human being has serious social, economic and political implications. Looking at our brother and sister and the whole of creation as a gift received from the love of the Father inspires attentive behavior, care and wonder. In this way the believer, contemplating his or her neighbor as a brother or sister, and not as a stranger, looks at him or her compassionately and empathetically, not contemptuously or with hostility. Contemplating the world in the light of faith, with the help of grace, we strive to develop our creativity and enthusiasm in order to resolve the ordeals of the past. We understand and develop our abilities as responsibilities that arise from this faith,[6] as gifts from God to be placed at the service of humanity and of creation.

While we all work for a cure for a virus that strikes everyone without distinction, faith exhorts us to commit ourselves seriously and actively to combat indifference in the face of violations of human dignity. This culture of indifference that accompanies the throwaway culture: things that do not affect me, do not interest me. Faith always requires that we let ourselves be healed and converted from our individualism, whether personal or collective; party individualism, for example.

May the Lord "restore our sight" so as to rediscover what it means to be members of the human family. And may this sight be translated into concrete actions of compassion and respect for every person and of care and safeguarding of our common home.

---

[1]  See *Evangelii gaudium*, 53; *Laudato si'*, 22.
[2]  Pastoral constitution *Gaudium et spes*, 12.
[3]  *Address to the General Assembly of the United Nations* (2 October 1979).
[4]  *Address to the General Assembly of the United Nations* (5 October 1995).
[5]  See *Compendium of the Social Doctrine of the Church*, 157.
[6]  *Ibid.*

# 3. The preferential option for the poor and the virtue of charity

**Library of the Apostolic Palace**
19 August 2020*

Dear brothers and sisters, good day!

The pandemic has exposed the plight of the poor and the great inequality that reigns in the world. And the virus, while it does not distinguish between people, has found, in its devastating path, great inequalities and discrimination. And it has exacerbated them!

The response to the pandemic is therefore dual. On the one hand, it is essential to find a cure for this small but terrible virus, which has brought the whole world to its knees. On the other, we must also cure a larger virus, that of social injustice, inequality of opportunity, marginalization, and the lack of protection for the weakest. In this dual response for healing there is a choice that, according to the Gospel, cannot be lacking: the *preferential option for the poor*.[1] And this is not a political option; nor is it an ideological option, a party option … no. The preferential option for the poor is at the center of the Gospel. And the first to do this was Jesus; we heard this in the reading from the Letter to the Corinthians which was read at the beginning. Since He was rich, He made Himself poor to enrich us. He made Himself one of us and for this reason, at the center of the Gospel, there is this option, at the center of Jesus' proclamation.

Christ Himself, Who is God, despoiled Himself, making Himself similar to men; and he chose not a life of privilege, but he chose the condition of a servant (see *Phil* 2:6–7). He annihilated Himself by making Himself a servant. He was born into a humble family and worked as a craftsman. At the beginning of His preaching, He announced that in the Kingdom of God the poor are blessed (see *Mt* 5:3; *Lk* 6:20; *Evangelii gaudium*, 197). He stood among the sick, the poor, the excluded, showing them God's merciful love.[2] And many times He was judged an impure man because He went to the sick, to lepers … and this made people impure, according to the law of the age. And He took risks to be near to the poor.

Therefore, Jesus' followers recognize themselves by their closeness to the poor, the little ones, the sick and the imprisoned, the excluded and the forgotten, those without food and clothing (see *Mt* 25:31–36; *CCC*, 2443). We can read that famous protocol by which we will all be judged, we

* http://www.vatican.va/content/francesco/en/audiences/2020/documents/papa-francesco_20200819_udienza-generale.html

will all be judged. It is Matthew, chapter 25. This is a *key criterion of Christian authenticity* (see *Gal* 2:10; *Evangelii gaudium*, 195). Some mistakenly think that this preferential love for the poor is a task for the few, but in reality it is the mission of the Church as a whole, as Saint John Paul II said.[3] "Each individual Christian and every community is called to be an instrument of God for the liberation and promotion of the poor society."[4]

Faith, hope and love necessarily push us towards this preference for those most in need,[5] which goes beyond necessary assistance.[6] Indeed it implies walking together, letting ourselves be evangelized by them, who know the suffering Christ well, letting ourselves be "infected" by their experience of salvation, by their wisdom and by their creativity.[7] Sharing with the poor means mutual enrichment. And, if there are unhealthy social structures that prevent them from dreaming of the future, we must work together Healing them, to change them.[8] And we are led to this by the love of Christ, Who loved us to the extreme (see *Jn* 13:1), and reaches the boundaries, the margins, the existential frontiers. Bringing the peripheries to the center means focusing our life on Christ, Who "made Himself poor" for us, to enrich us "by His poverty" (*2 Cor* 8:9),[9] as we have heard.

We are all worried about the social consequences of the pandemic. All of us. Many people want to return to normality and resume economic activities. Certainly, but this "normality" should not include social injustices and the degradation of the environment. The pandemic is a crisis, and we do not emerge from a crisis the same as before: either we come out of it better, or we come out of it worse. We must come out of it better, to counter social injustice and environmental damage. Today we have an opportunity to build something different. For example, we can nurture an economy of the integral development of the poor, and not of providing assistance. By this I do not wish to condemn assistance: aid is important. I am thinking of the voluntary sector, which is one of the best structures of the Italian Church. Yes, aid does this, but we must go beyond this, to resolve the problems that lead us to provide aid. An economy that does not resort to remedies that in fact poison society, such as profits not linked to the creation of dignified jobs.[10] This type of profit is dissociated from the real economy, that which should bring benefits to the common people,[11] and in addition is at times indifferent to the damage inflicted to our common home. The preferential option for the poor, this ethical-social need that comes from God's love,[12] inspires us to conceive of and design an economy where people, and especially the poorest, are at the center. And it also encourages us to plan the treatment of viruses by prioritizing those who are most in need. It would be sad if, for the vaccine for Covid-19, priority were to be given to the richest! It would be sad if this vaccine were to become the property of this nation or another, rather than universal and for all. And what a scandal it would be if all the economic assistance we are observing – most of it with public money – were to focus on rescuing those industries that do not contribute to the inclusion of the excluded, the promotion of the least, the common good or the care of creation.[13] There are criteria for choosing which industries should be helped: those which contribute to the inclusion of the excluded, to the promotion of the last, to the common good and the care of creation. Four criteria.

If the virus were to intensify again in a world that is unjust to the poor and vulnerable, then we must change this world. Following the example of Jesus, the doctor of integral divine love, that is, of physical, social and spiritual healing (see *Jn* 5:6–9) – like the healing worked by Jesus – we must act now, Healing the epidemics caused by small, invisible viruses, and to heal those caused by the great and visible social injustices. I propose that this be done by starting from the love of God, placing the peripheries at the center and the last in first place. Do not forget that protocol by which we will be judged, Matthew, chapter 25. Let us put it into practice in this recovery from the epidemic. And starting from this tangible love – as the Gospel says, there – anchored in hope and founded in faith, a healthier world will be possible. Otherwise, we will come out of the crisis worse. May the Lord help us, and give us the strength to come out of it better, responding to the needs of today's world. Thank you.

[1] See *Evangelii gaudium*, 195.

[2] See *Catechism of the Catholic Church*, 2444.

[3] See St. JOHN PAUL II, Encyclical letter *Sollicitudo rei socialis*, 42.

[4] *Evangelii gaudium*, 187.

[5] See CONGREGATION FOR THE DOCTRINE OF THE FAITH, *Instruction on some aspects of "Liberation Theology,"* (1984), chap. V.

[6] See *Evangelii gaudium*, 198.

[7] See *ibid*.

[8] See *ibid*, 195.

[9] BENEDICT XVI, *Address at the Inaugural Session of the Fifth General Conference of the Bishops of Latin America and the Caribbean*, 13 May 2007.

[10] See *Evangelii gaudium*, 204.

[11] See *Laudato si'*, 109.

[12] See *Laudato si'*, 158.

[13] *Ibid*.

# 4. The universal destination of goods and the virtue of hope

**Library of the Apostolic Palace**
26 august 2020*

Dear Brothers and Sisters, Good morning!

In the face of the pandemic and its social consequences, many risk losing hope. In this time of uncertainty and anguish, I invite everyone to welcome the gift of *hope* that comes from Christ. It is He who helps us navigate the tumultuous waters of sickness, death and injustice, which do not have the last word over our final destination.

The pandemic has exposed and aggravated social problems, above all that of inequality. Some people can work from home, while this is impossible for many others. Certain children, notwithstanding the difficulties involved, can continue to receive an academic education, while this has been abruptly interrupted for many, many others. Some powerful nations can issue money to deal with the crisis, while this would mean mortgaging the future for others.

These symptoms of inequality reveal a social illness; it is a virus that comes from a sick economy. And we must say it simply: the economy is sick. It has become ill. It is the fruit of unequal economic growth – this is the illness: the fruit of unequal economic growth – that disregards fundamental human values. In today's world, a few wealthy people possess more than all the rest of humanity. I will repeat this so that it makes us think: a few wealthy people, a small group, possess more than all the rest of humanity. This is pure statistics. This is an injustice that cries out to heaven! At the same time, this economic model is indifferent to the damage inflicted on our common home. Care is not being taken of our common home. We are close to exceeding many limits of our wonderful planet, with serious and irreversible consequences: from the loss of biodiversity and climate change to rising sea levels and the destruction of the tropical forests. Social inequality and environmental degradation go together and have the same root:[1] the sin of wanting to possess and wanting to dominate over one's brothers and sisters, of wanting to possess and dominate nature and God himself. But this is not the design for creation.

"In the beginning God entrusted the earth and its resources to the common stewardship of mankind to take care of them."[2] God has called us to dominate the earth in his name (see *Gn* 1:28), tilling it and keeping it like a garden, everyone's garden (see *Gn* 2:15). "'Tilling' refers to cultiva-

* http://www.vatican.va/content/francesco/en/audiences/2020/documents/papa-francesco_20200826_udienza-generale.html

ting, ploughing or working, while 'keeping' means caring, protecting, overseeing and preserving."[3] But be careful not to interpret this as a carte blanche to do whatever you want with the earth. No. There exists a "relationship of mutual responsibility"[4] between ourselves and nature. A relationship of mutual responsibility between ourselves and nature. We receive from creation and we give back in return. "Each community can take from the bounty of the earth whatever it needs for subsistence, but it also has the duty to protect the earth."[5] It goes both ways.

In fact, the earth "was here before us and it has been given to us,"[6] it has been given by God "for the whole human race."[7] And therefore it is our duty to make sure that its fruit reaches everyone, not just a few people. And this is a key element of our relationship with earthly goods. As the Fathers of the Second Vatican Council recalled, they said: "Man should regard the external things that he legitimately possesses not only as his own but also as common in the sense that they should be able to benefit not only him but also others."[8] In fact, "the ownership of any property makes its holder a steward of Providence, with the task of making it fruitful and communicating its benefits to others."[9] We are administrators of the goods, not masters. Administrators. "Yes, but the good is mine": that is true, it is yours, but to administer it, not to possess it selfishly for yourself.

To ensure that what we possess brings value to the community, "political authority has the right and duty to regulate the legitimate exercise of the right to ownership for the sake of the common good."[10] The "subordination of private property to the *universal destination of goods*, … is a golden rule of social conduct and the first principle of the whole ethical and social order."[11]

Property and money are instruments that can serve mission. However, we easily transform them into ends, whether individual or collective. And when this happens, essential human values are affected. The *homo sapiens* is deformed and becomes a species of *homo œconomicus* – in a detrimental sense – a species of man that is individualistic, calculating and domineering. We forget that, being created in the image and likeness of God, we are social, creative and solidary beings with an immense capacity to love. We often forget this. In fact, from among all the species, we are the beings who are the most cooperative and we flourish in community, as is seen well in the experience of the saints. There is a saying in Spanish that inspired me to write this phrase. It says: "*Florecemos en racimo, como los santos*": we flourish in community, as is seen well in the experience of the saints.[12]

When the obsession to possess and dominate excludes millions of persons from having primary goods; when economic and technological inequality are such that the social fabric is torn; and when dependence on unlimited material progress threatens our common home, then we cannot stand by and watch. No, this is distressing. We cannot stand by and watch! With our gaze fixed on Jesus (see *Heb* 12:2) and with the certainty that His love is operative through the community of His disciples, we must act all together, in the hope of generating something different and better. Christian hope, rooted in God, is our anchor. It moves the will to share, strengthening our mission as disciples of Christ, who shared everything with us.

The first Christian communities understood this. They lived difficult times, like us. Aware that they formed one heart and one soul, they put all of their goods in common, bearing witness to Christ's abundant grace in them (see *Acts* 4:32–35). We are experiencing a crisis. The pandemic has put us all in crisis. But let us remember that after a crisis a person is not the same. We come out of it better, or we come out of it worse. This is our option. After the crisis, will we continue with this economic system of social injustice and depreciating care for the environment, for creation, for our common home? Let's think about this. May the Christian communities of the twenty-first century recuperate this reality – care for creation and social justice: they go together – thus bearing witness to the Lord's Resurrection. If we take care of the goods that the Creator gives us, if we put what we possess in common in such a way that no one would be lacking, then we would truly inspire hope to regenerate a more healthy and equal world.

And in conclusion, let us think about the children. Read the statistics: how many children today are dying of hunger because of a non-good distribution of riches, because of the economic system as I said above; and how many children today do not have the right to education for the same reason. May this image of children in want due to hunger and the lack of education help us understand that after this crisis we must come out of it better. Thank you.

1 See *Laudato si'*, 101.

2 *Catechism of the Catholic Church*, 2402.

3 *Laudato si'*, 67.

4 *Ibid.*

5 *Ibid.*

6 *Ibid.*

7 *Catechism of the Catholic Church*, 2402.

8 *Gaudium et spes*, 69.

9 *Catechism of the Catholic Church*, 2404.

10 *Ibid.*, 2406. See *Gaudium et spes*, 71; St. John Paul II, Encyclical letter *Sollicitudo rei socialis*, 42; Encyclical letter *Centesimus Annus*, 40; 48.

11 *Laudato si'*, 93. See St. John Paul II, Encyclical letter *Laborem exercens*, 19.

12 *"Florecemos en racimo, como los santos"* (*We bloom in clusters, like the saints*): a popular expression in Spanish.

# 5. Solidarity and the virtue of faith

**San Damaso courtyard**
2 September 2020*

Dear Brothers and Sisters, good morning!

After many months, we meet each other again face to face, not screen to screen. Face to face. This is good! The current pandemic has highlighted our interdependence: we are all connected to each other, for better or for worse. Therefore, to emerge from this crisis better than before, we have to do so together; together, not alone. Together. Not alone, because it cannot be done. Either it is done together, or it is not done. We must do it together, all of us, in *solidarity*. I would like to underline this word today: *solidarity*.

As a human family we have our common origin in God; we live in a common home, the garden-planet, the earth where God placed us; and we have a common destination in Christ. But when we forget all this, our *interdependence* becomes *dependence* of some on others – we lose this harmony of interdependence and solidarity – increasing inequality and marginalization; the social fabric is weakened and the environment deteriorates. The same way of acting.

Therefore, the *principle of solidarity* is now more necessary than ever, as Saint John Paul ii taught.[1] In an interconnected world, we experience what it means to live in the same "global village"; this expression is beautiful. The big wide world is none other than a global village, because everything is interconnected, but we do not always transform this *interdependence* into *solidarity*. There is a long journey between interdependence and solidarity. The selfishness – of individuals, nations and of groups with power – and ideological rigidities instead sustain "structures of sin."[2]

"The word 'solidarity' is a little worn and at times poorly understood, but it refers to something more than a few sporadic acts of generosity." Much more! "It presumes the creation of a new mindset which thinks in terms of community and the priority of the life of all over the appropriation of goods by a few."[3] This is what "solidarity" means. It is not merely a question of helping others – it is good to do so, but it is more than that – it is a matter of justice.[4] Interdependence, to be in solidarity and to bear fruit, needs strong roots in humanity and in nature, created by God; it needs respect for faces and for the land.

* http://www.vatican.va/content/francesco/en/audiences/2020/documents/papa-francesco_20200902_udienza-generale.html

The Bible, from the very beginning, warns us [of this]. Let us think of the account of the Tower of Babel (see *Gen* 11:1–9), which describes what happens when we try to reach heaven – our destination – ignoring our bond with humanity, with creation and with the Creator. It is a figure of speech. This happens every time that someone wants to climb up and up, without taking others into consideration. Just myself. Let us think about the tower. We build towers and skyscrapers, but we destroy community. We unify buildings and languages, but we mortify cultural wealth. We want to be masters of the Earth, but we ruin biodiversity and ecological balance. In another audience I told you about those fishermen from San Benedetto del Tronto, who came this year, and said: "We have taken 24 tons of waste out of the sea, half of which was plastic." Just think! These people have the spirit to catch fish, yes, but also the refuse, and to take it out of the water to clean up the sea. But this [pollution] is ruining the earth – not having solidarity with the earth, which is a gift – and the ecological balance.

I remember a medieval account that describes this "Babel syndrome," which occurs when there is no solidarity. This medieval account says that, during the building of the tower, when a man fell – they were slaves – and died, no one said anything, or at best, "Poor thing, he made a mistake and he fell." Instead, if a brick fell, everyone complained. And if someone was to blame, he was punished. Why? Because a brick was costly to make, to prepare, to fire. … It took time and work to produce a brick. A brick was worth more than a human life. Let us each, think about what happens today. Unfortunately, something like this can happen nowadays too. When shares fall in the financial markets – we have seen it in the newspapers in these days – all the agencies report the news. Thousands of people fall due to hunger and poverty and no one talks about it.

Pentecost is diametrically opposite to Babel (see *Acts* 2:1–3), as we heard at the beginning of the audience. The Holy Spirit, descending from above like wind and fire, sweeps over the community closed up in the Cenacle, infuses it with the power of God, and inspires it to go out and announce the Lord Jesus to everyone. The Spirit creates unity in diversity; he creates harmony. In the account of the Tower of Babel, there was no harmony; only pressing forward in order to earn. There, people were simply instruments, mere "manpower," but here, in Pentecost, each one of us is an instrument, but a community instrument that participates fully in building up the community. Saint Francis of Assisi knew this well, and inspired by the Spirit, he gave all people, or rather, creatures, the name of brother or sister.[5] Even brother wolf, remember.

With Pentecost, God makes himself present and inspires the *faith* of the community *united in diversity and in solidarity*. Diversity and solidarity united in harmony, this is the way. A diversity in solidarity possesses "antibodies" that ensure that the singularity of each person – which is a gift, unique and unrepeatable – does not become sick with individualism, with selfishness. Diversity in solidarity also possesses antibodies that heal social structures and processes that have degenerated into systems of injustice, systems of oppression.[6] Therefore, solidarity today is the road to take towards a post-pandemic world, towards the healing of our interpersonal and social ills. There is no other way. Either we go forward on the path of solidarity, or things will worsen. I want to repeat this: one does not emerge from a crisis the same as before. The pandemic is a crisis. We emerge from a crisis either better or worse than before. It is up to us to choose. And solidarity is, indeed, a way of coming out of the crisis better, not with superficial changes, with a fresh coat of paint so everything looks fine. No. Better!

In the midst of crises, a *solidarity* guided by *faith* enables us to translate the love of God in our globalized culture, not by building towers or walls – and how many walls are being built today! – that divide, but then collapse, but by interweaving communities and sustaining processes of growth that are truly human and solid. And to do this, solidarity helps. I would like to ask a question: do I think of the needs of others? Everyone, answer in your heart.

In the midst of crises and tempests, the Lord calls to us and invites us to reawaken and activate this solidarity capable of giving solidity, support and meaning to these hours in which everything seems to be wrecked. May the creativity of the Holy Spirit encourage us to generate new forms of familiar hospitality, fruitful fraternity and universal solidarity. Thank you.

[1] See *Sollicitudo rei socialis,* 38-40.

[2] *Ibid.*, 36.

[3] *Evangelii gaudium*, 188.

[4] See *Catechism of the Catholic Church*, 1938–1949.

[5] See *Laudato si'*, 11; St. Bonaventure, *Legenda maior*, VIII, 6: *Franciscan Sources* 1145.

[6] See *Compendium of the Social Doctrine of the Church*, 192.

# 6. Love and the common good

**San Damaso courtyard**
9 September 2020*

Dear Brothers and Sisters, Good morning,

The crisis we are living due to the pandemic is affecting everyone; we will emerge from it for the better if we all seek the *common good* together; otherwise, we will emerge for the worse. Unfortunately, we see partisan interests emerging. For example, some would like to appropriate possible solutions for themselves, as in the case of vaccines, to then sell them to others. Some are taking advantage of the situation to instigate division: by seeking economic or political advantages, generating or exacerbating conflicts. Others are simply not concerned about the suffering of others; they pass by and go their own way (see *Lk* 10:30–32). They are the devotees of Pontius Pilate, washing their hands of the suffering of others.

The Christian response to the pandemic and to the consequent socioeconomic crisis is based on *love*, above all, love of God who always precedes us (see *1 Jn* 4:19). He loves us first. He always precedes us in love and in solutions. He loves us unconditionally and when we welcome this divine love, then we can respond similarly. I love not only those who love me – my family, my friends, my group – but also those who do not love me, I also love those who do not know me and I also love those who are strangers, and even those who make me suffer or whom I consider enemies (see *Mt* 5:44).

This is Christian wisdom, this is the attitude of Jesus. And the highest point of holiness, let's put it that way, is to love one's enemies, which is not easy. Certainly, to love everyone, including enemies, is difficult. I would say it is an art! But an art that can be learned and improved. True love that makes us fruitful and free is always expansive and inclusive. This love cares, heals and does good. Often, a caress does more good than many arguments, a caress of pardon instead of many arguments to defend oneself. It is inclusive love that heals.

So, *love* is not limited to the relationship between two or three people, or to friends or to family, it goes beyond. It comprises civil and political relationships,[1] including the relationship with nature.[2] Since we are social and political beings, one of the highest expressions of love is specifically social and political, which is decisive for human development and in order to face any type of crisis.[3]

* http://www.vatican.va/content/francesco/en/audiences/2020/documents/papa-francesco_20200909_udienza-generale.html

We know that love makes families and friendships flourish; but it is good to remember that it also makes social, cultural, economic and political relationships flourish, allowing us to construct a "civilization of love," as Saint Paul VI loved to say[4] and, in turn, Saint John Paul II. Without this inspiration the egotistical, indifferent, throw-away culture prevails – that is, to discard anyone I do not like, whom I cannot love or those who seem to me as not useful in society.

Today at the entrance, a couple said to me: "Pray for us because we have a disabled son" I asked: "How old is he?" – "He is pretty old" – "And what do you do?" – "We accompany him, we help him." All of their lives as parents for that disabled son. This is love. And the enemies, the political adversaries, according to our opinion appear to be politically and socially disabled, but they seem to be that way. Only God knows whether they truly are or not. But we must love them, we must dialogue, we must build this civilization of love, this political and social civilization of the unity of all humanity. All of this is the opposite of war, division, envy, even wars in families: inclusive love is social, it is familial, it is political ... love pervades everything!

The coronavirus is showing us that each person's true good is a common good, not only individual, and, vice versa, the common good is a true good for the person.[5] If a person only seeks his or her own good, that person is selfish. Instead, a person is more of a person when his or her own good is open to everyone, when it is shared. Health, in addition to being an individual good, is also a public good. A healthy society is one that takes care of everyone's health.

A virus that does not recognize barriers, borders, or cultural or political distinctions must be faced with a love without barriers, borders or distinctions. This love can generate social structures that encourage us to share rather than to compete, that allow us to include the most vulnerable and not to cast them aside, and that help us to express the best in our human nature and not the worst. True love does not know the throw-away culture, it does not know what it is. In fact, when we love and generate creativity, when we generate trust and solidarity, it is then that concrete initiatives for the common good emerge.[6]

And this is true at both the level of the smallest and largest communities, as well as at the international level. What is done in the family, what is done in the neighborhood, what is done in the village, what is done in the large cities and internationally is the same; it is the same seed that grows and bears fruit. If you in your family, in your neighborhood start out with envy, with fights, there will be "war" in the end. Instead, if you start out with love, sharing love, forgiveness, there will be love and forgiveness for everyone.

Conversely, if the solutions for the pandemic bear the imprint of egoism, whether it be by persons, businesses or nations, we may perhaps emerge from the coronavirus crisis, but certainly not from the human and social crisis that the virus has brought to light and exacerbated. Therefore, be careful not to build on sand (see *Mt* 7:21–27)! To build a healthy, inclusive, just and peaceful society we must do so on the rock of the common good.[7] The common good is a rock. And this is everyone's task, not only that of a few specialists. Saint Thomas Aquinas used to say that the promotion of the common good is a duty of justice that falls on each citizen. Every citizen is responsible for the common good. And for Christians, it is also a mission. As Saint Ignatius of Loyola taught, to direct our daily efforts toward the common good is a way of receiving and spreading God's glory.

Unfortunately, politics does not often have a good reputation, and we know why. This is not to say that all politicians are bad, no, I do not want to say this. I am only saying that unfortunately, politics does not often have a good reputation. But we should not resign ourselves to this negative vision, but instead react to it by showing in deeds that good politics is possible, indeed dutiful,[8] one that puts the human person and the common good at the center. If you read the history of humanity you will find many holy politicians who trod this path. It is possible insofar as every citizen, and especially those who assume social and political commitments and positions, root their action in ethical principles and nurture it with social and political love. Christians, in a particular way the lay faithful, are called to give a good example of this and can do so thanks to the virtue of charity, cultivating its intrinsic social dimension.

It is therefore time to improve our social love – I want to highlight this: our social love – with everyone's contribution, starting from our littleness. The common good requires everyone's participation. If everyone contributes his or her part, and if no one is left out, we can regenerate good relationships on the community, national and international level and even in harmony with the environment.[9] Thus, through our gestures, even the humblest ones, something of the image of God we bear within us will be made visible, because God is the Trinity, God is love. This is the most beautiful definition of God that is in the Bible. The Apostle John, who loved Jesus so much, gives it to us. With His help, we can *heal the world* working all together for the *common good*, not only for our own good but for the common good of all.

---

[1] See *Catechism of the Catholic Church*, 1907–1912.
[2] See *Laudato si'*, 231.
[3] *Ibid.*, 231.
[4] *Message for the 10th World Day of Peace*, 1 January 1977.
[5] See *Catechism of the Catholic Church*, 1905–1906.
[6] See St. John Paul II, Encyclical letter *Sollicitudo rei socialis*, 38.
[7] *Ibid.*, 10.
[8] See *Message for World Day of Peace*, 1 January 2019.
[9] See *Laudato si'*, 236.

# 7. Care of the common home and contemplative dimension

**San Damaso courtyard**
16 September 2020*

Dear Brothers and Sisters, Good morning!

To emerge from a pandemic, we need to look after and care for each other. And we must support those who care for the weakest, the sick and the elderly. There is the tendency to cast the elderly aside, to abandon them: this is bad. These people – well defined by the Spanish term *cuidadores* (caretakers), those who take care of the sick – play an essential role in today's society, even if they often do not receive the recognition and recompense they deserve. Caring is a golden rule of our nature as human beings, and brings with it health and hope.[1] Taking care of those who are sick, of those who are in need, of those who are cast aside: this is a human and also Christian wealth.

We must also extend this care to our common home: to the earth and to every creature. All forms of life are interconnected,[2] and our health depends on that of the ecosystems that God created and entrusted to us to care for (see *Gn* 2:15). Abusing them, on the other hand, is a grave sin that damages, harms and sickens.[3] The best antidote against this misuse of our common home is contemplation.[4] But why? Isn't there a vaccine for this, for the care of our common home, so as not to set it aside? What is the antidote against the sickness of not taking care of our common home? It is contemplation. "If someone has not learned to stop and admire something beautiful, we should not be surprised if he or she treats everything as an object to be used and abused without scruple."[5] Also in terms of "disposable" objects. However, our common home, creation, is not a mere "resource." Creatures have a value in themselves and each one "reflects in its own way a ray of God's infinite wisdom and goodness."[6] This value and this ray of divine light must be discovered and, in order to discover it, we need to be silent; we need to listen; we need to contemplate. Contemplation also heals the soul.

Without contemplation, it is easy to fall prey to an unbalanced and arrogant anthropocentrism, the "I" at the center of everything, which overinflates our role as human beings, positioning us as absolute rulers of all other creatures. A distorted interpretation of biblical texts on creation has contributed to this misinterpretation, which leads to the exploitation of the earth to the point of suffocating it. Exploiting creation: this is the sin. We believe we are at the center, claiming to occu-

---

* http://www.vatican.va/content/francesco/en/audiences/2020/documents/papa-francesco_20200916_udienza-generale.html

py God's place and so we ruin the harmony of creation, the harmony of God's plan. We become predators, forgetting our vocation as custodians of life. Of course, we can and must work the earth so as to live and to develop. But work is not synonymous with exploitation, and it is always accompanied by care: ploughing and protecting, working and caring. … This is our mission (see *Gn* 2:15). We cannot expect to continue to grow on a material level, without taking care of the common home that welcomes us. Our poorest brothers and sisters and our mother earth groan for the damage and injustice we have caused, and demand we take another course. They demand of us a conversion, a change of path; taking care of the earth too, of creation.

Therefore, it is important to recover the contemplative dimension, that is, to look at the earth, creation, as a gift, not as something to exploit for profit. When we contemplate, we discover in others and in nature something much greater than their usefulness. Here is the heart of the issue: contemplating is going beyond the usefulness of something. Contemplating the beautiful does not mean exploiting it: contemplating is free. We discover the intrinsic value of things given to them by God. As many spiritual masters have taught, the heavens, the earth, the sea, and every creature possess this iconic capacity, this mystical capacity to bring us back to the Creator and to communion with creation. For example, Saint Ignatius of Loyola, at the end of his Spiritual Exercises, invites us to carry out "Contemplation to attain love," that is, to consider how God looks at his creatures and to rejoice with them; to discover God's presence in his creatures and, with freedom and grace, to love and care for them.

Contemplation, which leads us to an attitude of care, is not a question of looking at nature from the outside, as if we were not immersed in it. But we are inside nature, we are part of nature. Rather, it is done from within, recognizing ourselves as part of creation, making us protagonists and not mere spectators of an amorphous reality that is only to be exploited. Those who contemplate in this way experience wonder not only at what they see, but also because they feel they are an integral part of this beauty; and they also feel called to guard it and to protect it. And there is one thing we must not forget: those who cannot contemplate nature and creation cannot contemplate people in their true wealth. And those who live to exploit nature end up exploiting people and treating them like slaves. This is a universal law. If you cannot contemplate nature it will be very difficult for you to contemplate people, the beauty of people, your brother, your sister.

Those who know how to contemplate will more easily set to work to change what produces degradation and damage to health. They will strive to educate and promote new habits of production and consumption, to contribute to a new model of economic growth that guarantees respect for our common home and respect for people. The contemplative in action tends to become a guardian of the environment: this is good! Each one of us should be a guardian of the environment, of the purity of the environment, seeking to combine ancestral knowledge of millennia-long cultures with new technical knowledge, so that our lifestyle may always be sustainable.

Lastly, *contemplating and caring*: these are two attitudes that show the way to correct and re-balance our relationship as human beings with creation. Oftentimes, our relationship with creation seems to be a relationship between enemies: destroying creation for our benefit. Exploiting creation for our profit. Let us not forget that this comes at a high price; let us not forget that Spanish saying: "God always forgives; we forgive sometimes; nature never forgives." Today I was reading in the newspaper about those two great glaciers in Antarctica, near the Amundsen Sea: they are about to fall. It will be terrible, because the sea level will rise and this will bring many, many difficulties and so much harm. And why? Because of global warming, not caring for the environment, not caring for our common home. On the other hand, when we have this relationship – let me say the word – "fraternal" in the figurative sense with creation, we will become guardians of our common home, guardians of life and guardians of hope; we will safeguard the patrimony that God has entrusted to us so that future generations may enjoy it. And some may say: "But, I can get by like this." But the problem is not how you are going to manage today – this was said by a German theologian, a Protestant, a good man: Bonhoeffer – the problem is not how you manage today; the problem is: what will be the legacy, life for future generations? Let us think of our children, our grandchildren: what will we leave them if we exploit creation? Let us protect this path so we may become "guardians" of our common home, guardians of life and hope. Let us safeguard the heritage that God has entrusted to us so that future generations may enjoy it. I think especially of the indigenous peoples, to whom we all owe a debt of gratitude, also of penance, to repair the harm we have done to them. But I am also thinking of those movements, associations, popular groups, that are committed to protecting their territory with its natural and cultural values. These social realities are not always appreciated; and at times they are even obstructed, because they do not earn money. But in reality, they contribute to a peaceful revolution: we might call it the "revolution of care." Contemplating so as to care, contemplating to protect, to protect ourselves, creation, our children, our grandchildren, and to protect the future. Contemplating to care for and to protect, and to leave a legacy to the future generation.

However, this must not be delegated to others: this is the task of every human being. Each one of us can and must be a "guardian of the common home," capable of praising God for his creatures, and of contemplating creatures, and protecting them. Thank you.

[1] See *Laudato si'*, 70.
[2] See *ibid.*, 137-138.
[3] See *Laudato si'*, 8; 66.
[4] See *ibid.*, 85; 214.
[5] *Ibid.*, 215.
[6] *Catechism of the Catholic Church*, 339.

# 8. Subsidiarity and virtue of hope

**San Damaso courtyard**
23 September 2020*

Dear Brothers and Sisters,

It seems the weather is not so good, but I wish you a good morning all the same!

To emerge better from a crisis like the current one, which is a health crisis, and at the same time, a social, political and economic crisis, each one of us is called to assume responsibility for our own part, that is, to share the responsibility. We must respond not only as individual people, but also beginning from the group to which we belong, from the role we have in society, from our principles and, if we are believers, from our faith in God. Often, however, many people cannot participate in the reconstruction of the common good because they are marginalized, they are excluded or ignored; some social groups are not able to make a contribution because they are economically or socially suffocated. In some societies, many people are not free to express their own faith and their own values, their own ideas: if they express them, they are put in jail. Elsewhere, especially in the western world, many people repress their ethical or religious convictions. However, we cannot emerge from the crisis this way, or at least emerge from it better. We would emerge from it worse.

So that we might be able to participate in the healing and regeneration of our peoples, it is only right that everyone should have the adequate resources to do so.[1] After the great economic depression of 1929, Pope Pius XI explained how important the *principle of subsidiarity* was.[2] This principle has a double movement: from top to bottom and from bottom to top. Perhaps we do not understand what this means, but it is a social principle that makes us more united. I will try to explain it.

On the one hand, and above all in moments of change, when single individuals, families, small associations and local communities are not capable of achieving primary objectives, it is right that the highest levels of society, such as the State, should intervene to provide the resources necessary to progress. For example, because of the coronavirus lockdown, many people, families and economic entities found themselves and still find themselves in serious difficulty. Thus,

* http://www.vatican.va/content/francesco/en/audiences/2020/documents/papa-francesco_20200923_udienza-generale.html

public institutions are trying to help through appropriate social, economic, health interventions: this is their function, what they need to do.

On the other hand, however, society's leaders must respect and promote the intermediate or lower levels. In fact, the contribution of individuals, of families, of associations, of businesses, of every intermediary body, and even of the Church, is decisive. With their own cultural, religious, economic resources, or civil participation, they revitalize and reinforce society.[3] That is, there is a collaboration from the top to the bottom, from the central State to the people, and from the bottom to the top: from the institutions of people to the top. And this is precisely how the principle of subsidiarity is exercised.

Everyone needs to have the possibility of assuming their own responsibility in the healing processes of the society of which they are a part. When a project is launched that directly or indirectly touches certain social groups, these groups cannot be left out from participating – for example: "What do you do?" – "I go to work with the poor," – "Beautiful. And what do you do?" – "I teach the poor, I tell the poor what they have to do." No, this doesn't work. The first step is to allow the poor to tell you how they live, what they need: Let everyone speak! And this is how the principle of subsidiarity works. We cannot leave the people out of participation; their wisdom, the wisdom of the humbler groups cannot be set aside.[4] Unfortunately, this injustice often happens in those places where there is a concentration of huge economic and geopolitical interests, such as, for example, certain extractive activities in some areas of the planet.[5] The voices of the indigenous peoples, their culture and world view are not taken into consideration.

Today, this lack of respect of the *principle of subsidiarity* has spread like a virus. Let us think of the great financial assistance measures enacted by States. The largest financial companies are listened to more than the people or the ones who really move the economy. Multinational companies are listened to more than social movements. Putting it in everyday language, the powerful are listened to more than the weak, and this is not the way, it is not the human way, it is not the way that Jesus taught us, it is not implementing the principle of subsidiarity. In this way, we do not permit people to be "agents in their own redemption."[6] There is this motto in the collective unconscious of some politicians or some trade unionists: everything for the people, nothing with the people. From top to bottom, but without listening to the wisdom of the people, without activating this wisdom in resolving problems, in this case in emerging from the crisis.

Or let us also think about the way to cure the virus: large pharmaceutical companies are listened to more than the healthcare workers employed on the front lines in hospitals or in refugee camps. This is not a good path. Everyone should be listened to, those who are at the top and those who are at the bottom, everyone.

To emerge better from a crisis, the *principle of subsidiarity* must be implemented, respecting everyone's autonomy and capacity to take initiative, especially that of the least. All the parts of a body are necessary, as Saint Paul says, those that may seem the weakest and least important, in reality are the most necessary (see *1 Cor* 12:22). In light of this image, we can say that the principle of subsidiarity allows everyone to assume his or her own role in the healing and destiny of society. Implementing it, implementing the principle of subsidiarity gives *hope*, it gives *hope* in a healthier and more just future; and we build this future together, aspiring to greater things, broadening our horizons.[7] Either we do it together, or it will not work. Either we work together to emerge from the crisis, at all levels of society, or we will never emerge from it. To emerge from the crisis does not mean to varnish over current situations so that they might appear more just. No. To emerge from the crisis means to change, and true change is done by everyone, all the persons that form a people. All the professions, all of them. And everything together, everyone in the community. If everyone does not contribute, the result will be negative.

In a previous catechesis we saw how *solidarity* is the way out of the crisis: it unites us and allows us to find solid proposals for a healthier world. But this path of solidarity needs *subsidiarity*. Someone might say to me: "But, Father, today you are using difficult words!" This is why I am trying to explain what it means. Showing solidarity because we are taking the path of subsidiarity. In fact, there is no true solidarity without social participation, without the contribution of intermediary bodies: families, associations, cooperatives, small businesses, and other expressions of society. Everyone needs to contribute, everyone. This type of participation helps to prevent and to correct certain negative aspects of globalization and government action, as also occurs in caring for the people affected by the pandemic. These contributions "from the bottom" should be encouraged. How beautiful it is to see the work of volunteers during the crisis. Volunteers from every part of society, volunteers who come from wealthier families and those from poorer families. But everyone, everyone together to emerge. This is solidarity and this is the principle of subsidiarity.

During the lockdown, the gesture of applauding doctors and nurses as a sign of encouragement and hope arose spontaneously. Many risked their lives and many gave their lives. Let us extend this applause to every member of the social body, to each and every one, for their precious contribution, no matter how small. "But what can that person over there do?" – "Listen to that person! Give the person space to work, consult him or her." Let us applaud the "discarded," those whom culture defines as "discarded," this throw-away culture – that is, let us applaud the elderly, children, persons with disability; let us applaud workers, all those who dedicate themselves to service; everyone collaborating to emerge from the crisis. But let us not stop only at applause. *Hope* is audacious, and so, let us encourage one another to dream big. Brothers and sisters, let us learn to dream big! Let us not be afraid to dream big, seeking the ideals of justice and social love that are born of hope. Let us not try to rebuild the past – the past is the past.

New things await us. The Lord promised: "I will make all things new." Let us encourage ourselves to dream big, seeking these ideals, let us not try to rebuild the past, especially the past that was unjust and already ill which I already mentioned as injustice. ... Let us build a future where the local and global dimensions mutually enrich each other – everyone can contribute, everyone has to contribute their share, their culture, their philosophy, their way of thinking – where beauty and the wealth of smaller groups, even those that are discarded, might flourish – because beauty is there too – and where those who have more dedicate themselves to service and give more to those who have less.

1 See *Compendium of the Social Doctrine of the Church*, 186.
2 See Encyclical letter *Quadragesimo anno*, 79–80.
3 See *Compendium of the Social Doctrine of the Church*, 185.
4 See Apostolic exhortation *Querida Amazonia*, 32; *Laudato si'*, 63.
5 See *ibid.*, 9; 14.
6 *Message for the 106th World Day of Migrants and Refugees 2020*, 13 May 2020.
7 See *Discourse to Students at the Fr. Félix Varela Cultural Center, Havana – Cuba*, 20 September 2015.

# 9. Preparing the future together with Jesus who saves and heals

**San Damaso courtyard**
30 September 2020*

Dear Brothers and Sisters, Good morning!

In recent weeks we have reflected together, in the light of the Gospel, on how Healing the world that is suffering from a malaise that has been highlighted and accentuated by the pandemic. The malaise was already there: the pandemic highlighted it more, it accentuated it. We have walked the paths of *dignity, solidarity* and *subsidiarity*, paths that are essential to promote human dignity and the *common good*. And as disciples of Jesus, we have proposed to follow in his steps, *opting for the poor, rethinking the use of material goods and taking care of our common home*. In the midst of the pandemic that afflicts us, we anchored ourselves to the principles of the *social doctrine of the Church*, allowing ourselves to be guided *by faith, by hope and by charity*. Here we found solid help so as to be transformers who dream big, who are not stopped by the meanness that divides and hurts, but who encourage the generation of a new and better world.

I would like this journey not to end with my catechesis, but rather that we may be able to continue to walk together, to "keep our eyes fixed on Jesus" (see *Heb* 12:2), as we heard at the beginning; our eyes fixed on Jesus, who saves and heals the world. As the Gospel shows us, Jesus healed the sick of every type (see *Mt* 9:35), he gave sight to the blind, the word to the mute, hearing to the deaf. And when he cured diseases and physical infirmity, he also healed the spirit by forgiving sins, because Jesus always forgives, as well as "social suffering" by including the marginalized.[1] Jesus, who renews and reconciles every creature (see *2 Cor* 5:17; *Col* 1:19–20), gives us the gifts necessary to love and heal as he knew how to do (see *Lk* 10:1–9; *Jn* 15:9–17), to take care of all without distinction on the basis of race, language or nation.

In order for this to really happen, we need to contemplate and appreciate the beauty of every human being and every creature. We were conceived in the heart of God (see *Eph* 1:3–5). "Each of us is the result of a thought of God. Each of us is willed, each of us is loved, each of us is necessary."[2] Furthermore, every creature has something to say to us about God the creator.[3] Acknowledging this truth and giving thanks for the intimate bonds in our universal communion with all people and all

---

* http://www.vatican.va/content/francesco/en/audiences/2020/documents/papa-francesco_20200930_udienza-generale.html

creatures activates "generous care, full of tenderness."[4] And it also helps us to recognize Christ present in our poor and suffering brothers and sisters, to encounter them and to listen to their cry and the cry of the earth that echoes it.[5]

Inwardly mobilized by these cries that demand of us another course,[6] that demand change, we will be able to contribute to the restoration of relations with our gifts and capacities.[7] We will be able to regenerate society and not return to so-called "normality," which is an ailing normality, indeed which was ailing before the pandemic: the pandemic highlighted it! "Now we return to normality": no, this will not do, because this normality was sick with injustice, inequality and environmental degradation. The normality to which we are called is that of the Kingdom of God, where "the blind receive their sight and the lame walk, lepers are cleansed, and the deaf hear, and the dead are raised up and the poor have good news preached to them" (*Mt* 11:5). And nobody plays dumb by looking the other way. This is what we have to do in order to change. In the normality of the Kingdom of God, there is bread for all and more to spare, social organization is based on contributing, sharing and distributing, not on possessing, excluding and accumulating (see *Mt* 14:13–21).

The gesture that enables progress in a society, a family, a neighborhood, or a city, everyone, is to give oneself, to give, which is not giving alms, but is a giving of self that comes from the heart. A gesture that distances us from selfishness and the anxiety of possessing. But the Christian way of doing this is not a mechanical way: it is a human way. We will never be able to emerge from the crisis that was highlighted by the pandemic, mechanically, with new tools – which are very important, they allow us to move forward, and we must not be afraid of them – but knowing that even the most sophisticated means, capable of doing many things, are incapable of one thing: tenderness. And tenderness is the very sign of Jesus' presence. Approaching others in order to walk [together], to heal, to help, to sacrifice oneself for others.

Thus, that normality of the Kingdom of God is important: that bread may reach everyone, that social organization be based on contributing, sharing and distributing, with tenderness; not on possessing, excluding and accumulating. Because at the end of life, we will not take anything with us into the other life!

A small *virus* continues to cause deep wounds and to expose our physical, social and spiritual vulnerabilities. It has laid bare the great inequality that reigns in the world: inequality of opportunity, of goods, of access to health care, of technology, education: millions of children cannot go to school, and so the list goes on. These injustices are neither natural nor inevitable. They are the work of man, they come from a model of growth detached from the deepest values. The waste of leftover food: with that waste one can feed everyone. And this has made many people lose hope and has increased uncertainty and anguish. This is why, to emerge from the pandemic, we must find the cure not only for the coronavirus – which is important! – but also for the great human and socioeconomic viruses. They must not be concealed by whitewashing them so that they cannot be seen. And certainly we cannot expect the economic model that underlies unfair and unsustainable development to solve our problems. It has not and will not do so, because it cannot do so, even though some false prophets continue to promise the "trickle-down effect" that never comes ("Trickle-down effect" in English, "*derrame*" in Spanish.[8]) You yourselves have heard the theory of the glass: the important thing is that the glass become full and then overflow to the poor and to others, and they receive wealth. But there is a phenomenon: the glass begins to fill up and when it is almost full it grows, it grows and grows, and the trickling down never happens. We must be careful.

We need to set to work urgently to generate good policies, to design systems of social organization that reward participation, care and generosity, rather than indifference, exploitation and particular interests. We must go ahead with tenderness. A fair and equitable society is a healthier society. A participatory society – where the "last" are taken into account just like the "first" – strengthens communion. A society where diversity is respected is much more resistant to any kind of virus.

Let us place this healing journey under the protection of the Virgin Mary, Our Lady of Health. May she, who carried Jesus in her womb, help us to be trustful. Inspired by the Holy Spirit, we can work together for the Kingdom of God that Christ inaugurated in this world by coming among us. It is a Kingdom of light in the midst of darkness, of justice in the midst of so many outrages, of joy in the midst of so much pain, of healing and of salvation in the midst of sickness and death, of tenderness in the midst of hatred. May God grant us to "viralize" *love* and to "globalize" *hope* in the light of *faith*.

[1] See *Catechism of the Catholic Church*, 1421.
[2] BENEDICT XVI, *Homily for the beginning of the Petrine ministry*, 24 April 2005; FRANCIS, *Laudato si'*, 65.
[3] See *Laudato si'*, 69, 239.
[4] *Ibid.*, 220.
[5] See *ibid.*, 49.
[6] See *ibid.*, 53.
[7] See *ibid.*, 19.
[8] See *Evangelii gaudium*, 54.

# Fratelli tutti

## Encyclical Letter on Fraternity and Social Friendship

3 October 2020*

The Encyclical Letter *Fratelli tutti* is a synthesis and a compendium of Pope Francis's teaching, and therefore, it is presented in its entirety as an analysis and a proposal for a new world. However, for the purposes of this collection, a few points are proposed directly from it that indicate the relationship that the heath crisis has in the Holy Father's teaching.

**7.** As I was writing this letter, the Covid-19 pandemic unexpectedly erupted, exposing our false securities. Aside from the different ways that various countries responded to the crisis, their inability to work together became quite evident. For all our hyper-connectivity, we witnessed a fragmentation that made it more difficult to resolve problems that affect us all. Anyone who thinks that the only lesson to be learned was the need to improve what we were already doing, or to refine existing systems and regulations, is denying reality.

**32.** True, a worldwide tragedy like the Covid-19 pandemic momentarily revived the sense that we are a global community, all in the same boat, where one person's problems are the problems of all. Once more we realized that no one is saved alone; we can only be saved together. As I said in those days, "the storm has exposed our vulnerability and uncovered those false and superfluous certainties around which we constructed our daily schedules, our projects, our habits and priorities. … Amid this storm, the façade of those stereotypes with which we camouflaged our egos, always worrying about appearances, has fallen away, revealing once more the ineluctable and blessed awareness that we are part of one another, that we are brothers and sisters of one another."[1]

**33.** The world was relentlessly moving towards an economy that, thanks to technological progress, sought to reduce "human costs"; there were those who would have had us believe that freedom of the market was sufficient to keep everything secure. Yet the brutal and unforeseen blow of this uncontrolled pandemic forced us to recover our concern for human beings, for everyone, rather than for the benefit of a few. Today we can recognize that "we fed ourselves on dreams of splendor

* http://www.vatican.va/content/francesco/en/encyclicals/documents/papa-francesco_20201003_enciclica-fratelli-tutti.html

and grandeur, and ended up consuming distraction, insularity and solitude. We gorged ourselves on networking, and lost the taste of fraternity. We looked for quick and safe results, only to find ourselves overwhelmed by impatience and anxiety. Prisoners of a virtual reality, we lost the taste and flavor of the truly real."[2] The pain, uncertainty and fear, and the realization of our own limitations, brought on by the pandemic have only made it all the more urgent that we rethink our styles of life, our relationships, the organization of our societies and, above all, the meaning of our existence.

**34.** If everything is connected, it is hard to imagine that this global disaster is unrelated to our way of approaching reality, our claim to be absolute masters of our own lives and of all that exists. I do not want to speak of divine retribution, nor would it be sufficient to say that the harm we do to nature is itself the punishment for our offences. The world is itself crying out in rebellion. We are reminded of the well-known verse of the poet Virgil that evokes the "tears of things," the misfortunes of life and history.[3]

**35.** All too quickly, however, we forget the lessons of history, "the teacher of life."[4] Once this health crisis passes, our worst response would be to plunge even more deeply into feverish consumerism and new forms of egotistic self-preservation. God willing, after all this, we will think no longer in terms of "them" and "those," but only "us." If only this may prove not to be just another tragedy of history from which we learned nothing. If only we might keep in mind all those elderly persons who died for lack of respirators, partly as a result of the dismantling, year after year, of healthcare systems. If only this immense sorrow may not prove useless, but enable us to take a step forward towards a new style of life. If only we might rediscover once for all that we need one another, and that in this way our human family can experience a rebirth, with all its faces, all its hands and all its voices, beyond the walls that we have erected.

**36.** Unless we recover the shared passion to create a community of belonging and solidarity worthy of our time, our energy and our resources, the global illusion that misled us will collapse and leave many in the grip of anguish and emptiness. Nor should we naively refuse to recognize that "obsession with a consumerist lifestyle, above all when few people are capable of maintaining it, can only lead to violence and mutual destruction."[5] The notion of "every man for himself" will rapidly degenerate into a free-for-all that would prove worse than any pandemic.

**54.** Despite these dark clouds, which may not be ignored, I would like in the following pages to take up and discuss many new paths of hope. For God continues to sow abundant seeds of goodness in our human family. The recent pandemic enabled us to recognize and appreciate once more all those around us who, in the midst of fear, responded by putting their lives on the line. We began to realize that our lives are interwoven with and sustained by ordinary people valiantly shaping the decisive events of our shared history: doctors, nurses, pharmacists, storekeepers and supermarket workers, cleaning personnel, caretakers, transport workers, men and women working to provide essential services and public safety, volunteers, priests and religious. ... They understood that no one is saved alone.[6]

**168.** The marketplace, by itself, cannot resolve every problem, however much we are asked to believe this dogma of neoliberal faith. Whatever the challenge, this impoverished and repetitive school of thought always offers the same recipes. Neoliberalism simply reproduces itself by resorting to the magic theories of "spillover" or "trickle" – without using the name – as the only solution to societal problems. There is little appreciation of the fact that the alleged "spillover" does not resolve the inequality that gives rise to new forms of violence threatening the fabric of society. It is imperative to have a proactive economic policy directed at "promoting an economy that favors productive diversity and business creativity"[7] and makes it possible for jobs to be created and not cut. Financial speculation fundamentally aimed at quick profit continues to wreak havoc. Indeed, "without internal forms of solidarity and mutual trust, the market cannot completely fulfil its proper economic function. And today this trust has ceased to exist."[8] The story did not end the way it was meant to, and the dogmatic formulae of prevailing economic theory proved not to be infallible. The fragility of world systems in the face of the pandemic has demonstrated that not everything can be resolved by market freedom. It has also shown that, in addition to recovering a sound political life that is not subject to the dictates of finance, "we must put human dignity back at the center and on that pillar build the alternative social structures we need."[9]

[1] *Extraordinary Moment of Prayer in Time of Epidemic, 27 March 2020.*

[2] *Homily in Skopje*, North Macedonia, 7 May 2019.

[3] See *Aeneid* 1, 462: "*Sunt lacrimae rerum et mentem mortalia tangent.*"

[4] "*Historia... magistra vitae*" (CICERO, *De Oratore*, 2,6).

[5] *Laudato si'*, 204.

[6] See *Extraordinary Moment of Prayer in Time of Epidemic*, 27 March 2020; *Message for the 2020 World Day of the Poor*, 13 June 2020, 6.

[7] *Laudato si'*, 129.

[8] BENEDICT XVI, Encyclical letter *Caritas in Veritate*, 35.

[9] *Address to Participants in the World Meeting of Popular Movements*, 28 October 2014.

# We live by remembering

We live by remembering

To remember is to live.

A memory refers to a past fact; the memory seizes it, history records it, tradition conserves it.

I think this is the meaning of this "memory album."

Memories of intense moments, that we all lived together with Pope Francis. Leaf through these pages and look back, remember.

Not only do we need to conserve an historic awareness of events that we never dreamed would occur, but we also need to learn how to face and accept the suffering of our lives.

These events have taught us that no one suffers alone.

No one suffers uselessly.

The powerful image of Pope Francis in the rain embracing the Crucifix of Saint Marcello's Church, reminds us that those who suffer with Christ.

The Cross is the sign of the Christian.

The height of Christian greatness.

On that evening, as on the evening of Good Friday, we experienced that suffering unites people as brothers and sisters, and where suffering is, the heart cannot be absent. Those who believe in God are near those who suffer.

Among the great wonders of our Christian faith is also that of the teaching regarding patient suffering and of discovering treasures of humanity and grace in suffering and misfortune.

If no man is an island; we are "Fratelli tutti", united in natural solidarity that derives from the common belonging to the human race; if especially we, followers of Christ, are united in the bond of charity, we cannot but suffer when others suffer.

Pope Francis's words are also an invitation to hope.

Hope is not a dream, but a way of translating dreams into reality.

The best emerges only with great pain.

Suffering passes; having suffered remains.

Out of suffering arises a new dawn.

We will once again enjoy life!

**Leonardo Sapienza**

# Prayer to Mary

O Mary, You shine continuously on our journey
as a sign of salvation and hope.
We entrust ourselves to you, Health of the Sick, who, at the Cross,
united with Jesus' pain, keeping your faith firm.
You, Salvation of the Roman people, know what we need,
and we trust that you will provide for those needs so that, as at Cana of Galilee,
joy and celebratimay return after this moment of trial.
Help us, Mother of Divine Love, to conform ourselves to the will of the Father
and to do what Jesus tells us. He who took our suffering upon Himself,
and burdened Himself with our sorrows to bring us, through the Cross,
to the joy of Resurrection. Amen.
Amen.

*We seek refuge under your protection, O Holy Mother of God.*
*Do not despise our pleas — we who are put to the test —*
*and deliver us from every danger. O glorious and blessed Virgin.*

* http://www.vatican.va/content/francesco/en/messages/pont-messages/2020/documents/papa-francesco_20200311_videomessaggio-madonna-divinoamore.html

**Icona di Maria *Salus Populi romani***
The Papal Basilica of Santa  Maria Maggiore

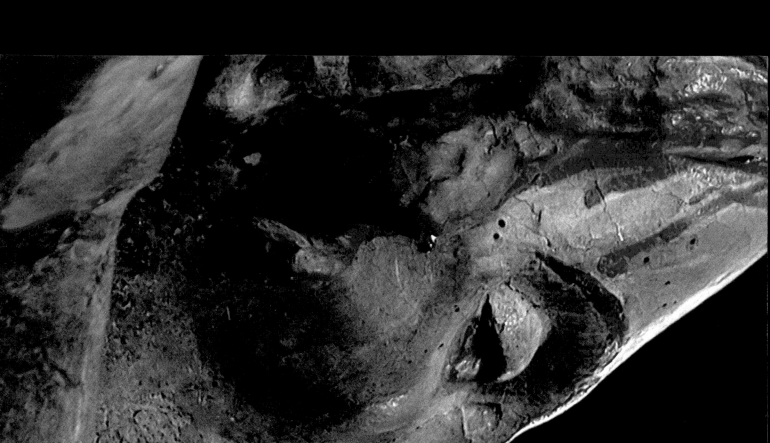

"porchè avete paura...
... non avete ancora fede"? (Mc. 4, 35-41)

Signore, benedici il mondo...

Francesco

"Why are you afraid? ...
... Have you no faith?" (*Mc* 4,35-41)

Lord, may you bless the world...

**Francis**

# Extraordinary Moment of Prayer
## in Time of Pandemic

https://e.va/statioorbisen

# Table of Contents

Part II

© Copyright 2021 - Libreria Editrice Vaticana
00120 Città del Vaticano
Tel (+39) 06.698.45780
E-mail: commerciale.lev@spc.va
www.libreriaeditricevaticana.va
www.vatican.va

© Bayard Éditions, 2021
18, Rue Barbes
92128 Montrouge Cedex (France)
Tel (+33) 01 74 31 59 98

ISBN 978-1-68192-962-0

© Our Sunday Visitor Publishing
Our Sunday Visitor, Inc.
200 Noll Plaza
Huntington, IN 46750
www.osv.com

1-800-348-2440

Completed printing in Slovenia in March 2021

Graphic and design project
Marcello Palminteri

Cover design
Annalaura di Luggo

**Annydi srl,** Napoli
www.annydi.com